KIMBERLY

JACK WEYLAND

Deseret Book Company
Salt Lake City, Utah

Library of Congress Cataloging-in-Publication Data

Weyland, Jack, 1940–
    Kimberly / Jack Weyland.
      p. cm.
    Summary: Twenty-one-year-old Ben falls in love with his singing
partner Kimberly but finds their relationship strained by the
divorce that is tearing apart her Mormon family.
    ISBN 0-87579-599-4
    [1. Divorce—Fiction. 2. Mormons—Fiction. 3. Christian life—
Fiction.] I. Title.
PZ7.W538Ki   1992
[Fic]—dc20   92-730
                                             CIP
                                             AC

Printed in the United States of America

10   9   8   7   6   5   4   3   2   1

1

Ben Fairbanks sat in a music practice room at the University of Utah on a cold January day, waiting for anyone else who might want to try out. He was looking for a female singer who played acoustic guitar and wanted to earn a little extra money on weekends. He fumbled on his guitar for a song that would change the world — or, if not that, at least help pay for college.

He heard what sounded like a cat scratching at the door. Glancing up, he saw a girl struggling to get through the door while balancing two college textbooks and a three-ring binder in one hand, a guitar case in the other. It was a great act, but it only lasted until she got inside. Then the books and binder crashed to the floor.

He hurried to help her. "Thanks for dropping in," he said. She was someone he would have noticed even across a crowded room. As she picked up loose papers that had fallen from her three-ring binder, he was fascinated by how graceful she was. It was as if she moved to a song that no one else could hear. Even though he knew she was embarrassed, she radiated a composure that only added to her beauty.

She turned to him and smiled. "I'm practicing dramatic entrances today. So, how'd I do?"

"Great. You got my attention." Which was true. He was intrigued by the color of her hair. He tried to recall when he'd seen that color before. Finally it dawned on him: he saw it every day at breakfast. It was the color of honey in the morning sun. Her perfume was subtle but unforgettable; it seemed to match her personality.

She held out her hand, palm up. He fantasized that she wanted him to hold it, but then he realized she just wanted her book back. He glanced down at the title. It was a calculus book. He got rid of it really fast.

"Thanks," she said. "I saw a notice on the bulletin board about a tryout here today. Are you the one I should talk to?"

"Yes. I'm Ben Fairbanks."

"Hi. I'm Kimberly Madison." She set her books on a desk, then took her guitar out of its case and began to tune it. "Your notice was sort of sketchy. You want to tell me what this is all about?"

"Yeah, sure. This summer I got off my mission with no money and not much time before fall semester began. I managed to make enough to get registered and buy books, but that's about all. The last part of September I ran into a girl I used to sing with in high school."

"What's her name?"

He cleared his throat. "Julia Alton. Do you know her?"

"No."

He was relieved she didn't know Julia. Maybe she hadn't heard anything. "Well, anyway, we worked up some songs and then went around town trying to find someone who'd pay us to sing. We finally lined up a job for Friday and Saturday nights at an Italian restaurant called Angelo's. Have you ever eaten there?"

"No, but I've heard of it."

"We sang every weekend until Christmas break, but then Julia got married over Christmas and moved away, so now I'm looking for someone to take her place. It's steady work, it pays well, and it doesn't interfere much with school. We put on a twenty-minute show three times a night from seven until ten Friday and Saturday nights. For that and mingling with the

2

customers, and once in a while, when they're really busy, waiting on a few tables, we each get seventy-five dollars a night."

"Sounds good." She tuned her guitar and then asked, "What would you like me to play for you?"

"Anything you want."

"Okay. I'll do a song I wrote and sang for my high school graduation."

"When was that?"

"A year ago last May."

Her hair in the back was in a French braid. He tried to imagine what it would be like to watch her braid it, but then, because of the problems he'd had with Julia and her boyfriend, he reminded himself that he needed to keep things with the new singer on a strictly professional basis. With that in mind, he quit fantasizing about Kimberly's hair.

She started singing. Her voice was clear and natural and vibrant, but it was her song that amazed him most of all.

"What do you think?" she asked when it was over.

"It sounds terrific. Are you majoring in music?"

"No, mechanical engineering. Music is just a hobby."

"Mechanical engineering? Gosh, I'm impressed."

"Don't be. It's just that math has always come easy for me. What are you majoring in?"

"Business. Music is sort of a hobby for me too. Look, I've got some sheet music for some of the songs Julia and I were doing. Why don't you look them over and find one you like, and we'll try singing it and see how it goes."

She picked out a song and they began singing. He was surprised how well they sounded together. When they finished, he said, "I think this might work out. Can you start this Friday?"

"I won't know enough songs by then."

"I know, but if we can get together tomorrow and Thursday, I think we can work up enough to get by."

"Okay, sure."

"After that we'll set up some regular practice sessions."

"Anything else I should know?" she asked.

"Just one thing." He paused. "That song you wrote, it's unbelievable. I can't get it out of my mind."

"You really liked it?"

"Absolutely. But even as good as it was, I do have a couple of suggestions for you—if you're interested."

"Okay."

"First of all, it's too good to only be sung once at a high school graduation," he said. "The lyrics need to grab everyone who hears it."

She crinkled up her nose. "Let me guess—you want to turn it into a love song, right?"

"Why not? Most people are either in love or else wish they were."

"I'm not in love and I don't wish I were," she said.

"Me either, but let's face it, we're the exceptions."

"All right, let's try it as a love song."

They changed the words first but that caused a change in part of the melody, so they ended up jockeying back and forth until finally they were both satisfied. "Let's try it together all the way through now, okay?" Ben suggested.

She stepped forward and addressed a large imaginary audience. "I know you'll all recognize this next song because it was our first big hit. We'd like to sing it for you now."

When they finished, she held up her hand to stop the thunderous applause of an imaginary audience. "Thank you, thank you! You've been a wonderful audience! Would you like us to sing it one more time?"

They did it again. For a moment, for them, there really was a sell-out audience shouting their approval.

When they were done, he sat down. "Here's a song I've been working on," he said. He played it, then asked, "So, what do you think?"

"I like it," she said, "but . . . what would you think about this?" She played a variation on his tune. It was better. And then he improved on her idea. And then suddenly it was like they were one person, working together, coming up with ideas for words and music they never could have done alone. It all seemed to take place in about ten minutes, but by the time they looked at the clock, an hour and a half had passed.

"I can't believe it's so late!" she said. "My mom's going to kill me."

"Can I give you a ride home?"

"Yeah, thanks. That would really help. I don't live very far from here."

"What happened just now doesn't happen every day. It's like by myself I'm only half a person, and you're the other half. We've got two great songs finished in just a day. I know we're both busy, but what if, in addition to practicing, we spent a little time each week writing some of our own songs?"

"What for?"

"We could make a tape to sell to the people who eat at Angelo's. Even if we only sell two or three a night, it will bring us in a little extra. And, who knows, someday we might make it big."

She didn't believe him. "Yeah, right."

"Hey, it's not that expensive to record a few songs in a studio. Say it costs four dollars a tape and we sell them for ten dollars — that gives us a profit of six dollars a tape. If we sell five a night, that's an extra thirty dollars a night."

"You're definitely in the right major."

As they pulled into her driveway, he looked at her and said, "Don't go in yet, okay? There's still a lot we need to talk about."

"Let me tell my folks I'm home first."

When she returned, she said, "My mom says you're welcome to come in and eat with me. Everyone else has eaten."

"Can't we just talk in the car?"

"You got something against eating? Look, if we're going to

5

talk, let's at least do it over food. You don't want me passing out from hunger, do you?"

"You're sure I won't be in the way?"

"Not a bit. We'll just be scraping the pan for whatever food my brother Derek left. Derek's my little brother. He's only fifteen, but he's a big guy and he eats a lot. Come on in. Don't be bashful."

"Nice house," he said as they went up the walk to the old two-story frame house.

"Thanks. When we bought it, it needed a lot of work. We fixed it up ourselves, and now it's the pride of the neighborhood. At least that's what my dad always says whenever he shows people around."

"I bet you made some hardware store owner happy when you were fixing it up. The reason I say that is, my dad runs a hardware store in Rock Springs, Wyoming. That's where I'm from."

She took him into the kitchen. "Mom, this is the guy who kidnapped me and wouldn't let me come home for supper. He told me his name is Ben Fairbanks, but of course I don't believe that for an instant."

"Ben, it's nice to meet you," Kimberly's mother, Anne Madison, said, holding out her hand to shake his.

Someone had once told Ben that if he wanted to know what a girl is going to look like someday, he should look at her mother. Ever since then, he had made it a practice to pay attention to the appearance of the mothers of the girls he spent time with. Even though he wasn't looking for a wife in Kimberly, mainly because of what had happened with Julia, he decided it wouldn't be so bad to be married to Kimberly if she looked as good as her mother in twenty years. Anne had brown eyes and brown hair with a little gray mixed in. To Ben she looked quietly competent and totally conscientious.

"Mrs. Madison, I apologize for making Kimberly late. We started working on a song and lost all track of the time."

"I'm just glad she's home. Look, there's not a lot of food here, but you're welcome to whatever you can find. As usual, Derek ate most of it." She got them started and then left.

A few minutes later, Derek came in for a snack. He was a big kid who was growing so fast it was hard to keep him in clothes. There was about an inch of open skin between the bottom of his T-shirt and his jeans. He had sandy hair, which his mother always insisted was too long, and an infectious smile that few could resist.

"Derek, this is Ben. He and I are going to be singing together at a pizza place Friday and Saturday nights."

"Bring some pizza home when you're done," Derek said, getting the jar of peanut butter from the cupboard.

"Derek is almost an Eagle scout," Kimberly said.

"That's really great, Derek!" Ben exclaimed.

"I just have to do my Eagle project and then I'll be done. Did you ever get your Eagle?"

"Yeah, just barely. If you need any help, let me know."

"It's mostly my dad who's pushing me to get it. Right now my main goal is to get strong enough to intimidate all the guys my age."

"I'd say you're about there," Ben said.

Derek smiled, then turned to Kimberly. "You'd better listen to this guy. And from now on, quit telling your friends I'm your little brother when I'm bigger than you."

"Derek, you'll always be my little brother. Oh, and tuck in your shirt. People don't like looking at your belly button."

Derek tucked in his shirt, sat down at the table with them, and started to make a peanut butter and jelly sandwich. "I'm not only getting stronger, but I can tell now that I'm going to be really hairy too."

"Oh my gosh, Derek," Kimberly complained, "give us a break. We're trying to eat."

"I wasn't talking to you." He turned to Ben. "Anyway, I'm going to be hairy, but not half as hairy as this guy I saw at the pool last summer. I'm serious. He had so much hair on his chest and his back, he looked like a gorilla. I hope I'm like that someday so that when little kids see me, like at a swimming pool, they'll start bawling and run to their mothers. A guy needs something like that going for him, right?"

"Sure, and a voice like Darth Vader," Ben said.

"Yes! Finally somebody around here understands what things are like for me. Having two sisters is tough. Like you would not believe the things they hang over the shower curtain in the bathroom."

"Derek, isn't there someplace you'd rather be now?" Kimberly cut in.

"No. Hey, Ben, do you think Kimberly's good looking?"

"The first time I saw her, it took my breath away."

"Yeah, well, you ought to see her in the morning when she first gets up—that'd take anybody's breath away." Derek made the desperate sound of someone struggling to breathe. "It's like that one scene from *Swamp Woman*, you know, the one where Swamp Woman comes out of the swamp with all this green crud hanging from her hair and a tour bus in her mouth."

"Derek?" Kimberly muttered.

"What?"

"Go away."

"Why should I?"

"We're busy."

"Oh yeah, right, I can see you're real busy."

"We need to talk about music."

"In a minute, okay? I'm not through with my sandwich yet." He took another bite and then turned to Kimberly. "See if you can talk Mom and Dad into getting us a computer."

"They have computers in school, don't they?" she asked.

"Yeah, but Mrs. Vitali is so afraid of them, she goes crazy when someone tries to use them. Like she comes up and goes, 'Be careful and don't push the wrong button and break it.'

8

Yeah, right, like somebody at the factory goes, 'Hey, I've got a great idea. Let's put a button on this thing so if anyone pushes it, the whole thing blows up.'" He took a big swig of milk. "People are so dumb. Sometimes I feel like I live in an insane asylum and just down the road is a place where normal people live except I don't know that. Thinking things like that can drive you crazy. But maybe that wouldn't be so bad. At least I'd fit in more. Well, I've got to get back to my room." He stood up to leave.

"I don't suppose you'd consider cleaning up the mess you made here, would you?" she asked.

"What mess?"

"Put away the peanut butter and the jelly. And wash your knife and glass."

"Why should I do that? That's women's work."

"Derek, how would you like me to go to your school and announce your middle name over the P.A. system?"

"You wouldn't do that."

"Not if you clean up."

Derek turned to Ben. "You see what it's like living around here? Take it from me, sisters are a pain."

After a half-hearted attempt to clean up, he spotted a basketball on the floor. He picked it up and became both announcer and player. "The game's tied, Madison has the ball, he races down the court and puts up a lay-up." He tossed the basketball into the kitchen sink. "It's good! The crowd goes wild! Aaaaahh!" He dribbled the ball up the stairs to his room.

"That's my brother Derek," she said.

"Nice guy."

She smiled. "That's easy for you to say. You don't have to live in the same house with him. I'm positive his goal is to make as much noise as possible."

"That's what a guy his age is supposed to do."

"Were you ever like that?"

"Sure, probably worse."

"Well, it's good to know there's still hope for him."

"It's fun getting to know your family."

"What's your family like?"

"I'm an only child. The doctors told my mother she'd never have kids, and then I came along—but I was the only one."

Kimberly's twelve-year-old sister Megan walked in. "Oh, I didn't know anyone else was here," she said.

"Megan, this is Ben. He plays the guitar too. We've got a job singing together this semester."

"Hello," Megan said.

"Hi, Megan. Gosh, you're as good-looking as your sister," Ben said, not so much as a compliment as a statement of fact. She had long brown hair and gray-blue eyes; her skin was an elegant ivory tone. She seemed more serious than Kimberly.

Megan, entranced by this tall, dark stranger, sat down.

"Don't you have some homework or something?" Kimberly asked.

"No."

"I bet you get really good grades, right?" Ben said.

Megan smiled. "Yeah, pretty much."

"And I bet there's guys in school wishing they had the courage to come up and talk to you."

"Not really."

"Hey, I'm hardly ever wrong about things like this."

Kimberly realized that Megan felt so comfortable with Ben that she might stay there for a long time. She tried to speed things up. "Megan, Ben and I need to talk."

Megan nodded her head and got up to leave.

"I enjoyed meeting you," Ben said.

"Me too." She left.

"Well, somehow you've managed to impress my family," Kimberly said.

"I really like them."

"We haven't talked much about music yet," she said.

"Is there someplace we can go where we won't be disturbed?"

"Downstairs. My dad used to have an office at home. He doesn't use it anymore. We could go there."

They went downstairs. The basement was unfinished, with a room built at one end. The room, which was carpeted, had a small desk, two chairs, and a filing cabinet. Kimberly plugged in a portable electric heater.

Ben moved the two chairs together and they sat down. "The first thing we need to do is work up some songs for Friday. And then after that, we'll need to practice two or three times a week, and if you have the time, it'd be great if we could get together once a week to write new songs. After we've got five or six new songs, we'll put together a tape. How does that sound?"

"Busy. You want to know what I'm taking this quarter? Calculus, chemistry, English, computer programming."

"Give me one hour a day, four days a week, that's all I ask."

"Okay, one hour, but that's all."

"Great. When's a good time for you?" he asked.

"How about four o'clock, Monday through Thursday?"

"Yeah, sure, that'll work." He paused, then cleared his throat. "There's something else we need to talk about."

"What's that?"

"We'll be spending a lot of time together, so it'd be best if we kept everything on a strictly professional basis."

"Are you worried about that?"

"I just don't want some silly romance to come from this. Physical attraction can be really distracting."

She smiled. "You make it sound like a disease." And then she stopped and stared at him. "Why are you telling me this anyway? Did you and Julia have a problem?"

"No, why? What have you heard?"

"What have I heard? What kind of a question is that? I

haven't heard anything, but you'd better level with me now or else get yourself another singer."

"Nothing happened between Julia and me, but the guy she was going with thought there was. I guess because we spent so much time together. Well, anyway, he started secretly following us. One night I invited Julia over to my apartment, just to talk. It was totally innocent. For one thing, I live in my aunt's house in an upstairs apartment. Anyway, Julia and I are in my apartment eating popcorn and watching TV when all of a sudden somebody starts banging on the door and yelling like a crazy man. Of course, my aunt is scared to death and won't even open the door, but it's not locked so he barges in and demands to know where Julia is. My aunt tells him and he runs up the stairs. He sees us together and starts shouting at us and accusing us of a lot of things that weren't true.

"While this is going on, my aunt calls the police. We try to reason with the guy but it's no use. Finally he gets so mad he grabs Julia and starts dragging her across the floor, telling her she's coming with him. But she doesn't want to go with him when he's like that. So anyway, I try to get him to let go of her. And then all of a sudden, it's like something snaps inside his head and he comes after me. We start fighting, and then the police show up. He's yelling at Julia and me as they drag him off to jail. The police let him cool off in a cell overnight. But when he gets out of jail, he goes back on campus and tells everyone a bunch of lies about what kind of a person I am. And then a month later Julia gets married."

"She ended up marrying him?" Kimberly asked.

"No, she married one of the cops who answered the call." He paused. "So you see, after all that, I'd really like to keep things low-key and professional."

He could tell she wasn't totally convinced. "Like you did with Julia, you mean?" she asked.

"Yeah, like I did with Julia. Look, if you have any questions about any of this, I'll give you Julia's phone number or you can talk to my aunt. I've got nothing to hide."

"No, that's okay, I believe you. All right, low-key and professional." She turned away. It gave him a good chance to look at her again.

She turned back to face him. "Why do you keep staring at me?" she asked.

"Was I staring at you?"

"Yes, you were. Why?"

"Well, there's some things about you . . . that I find attractive—but, of course, when we're working together, I won't even notice those things."

"What things won't you notice?" she asked.

"You want me to give you a list?"

"Sure, why not? Our relationship isn't going anywhere, so I don't have to worry about that. But I've always been curious about what guys notice when they see a girl."

"I'd really rather not talk about this," he said.

"I'm just curious, that's all. I promise I won't bring it up again. What did you think when you first saw me?"

"The first thing I noticed was your hair."

"What about it?"

"It's the same color as my honey in the morning."

Her smile vanished. "Oh . . . I see." She cleared her throat and moved her chair six inches farther away from him. "I didn't know. What is . . . your honey's name?"

At first he didn't know what she was talking about, but when he finally did, he gasped, "Oh no, nothing like that. What I meant is the honey I have with my toast in the morning."

They both laughed at the misunderstanding.

"What else?" she asked.

"You get freckles in the summer, don't you? I like that. In Wyoming there's two things we look for in a girl. One is freckles and the other is if she owns a quarter horse."

13

"One out of two isn't bad, is it? Maybe I should move to Wyoming."

"Sure, why not?"

"Do you want to know what girls find attractive about you?"

"No," he said quickly.

"You do too, Ben, you liar."

"I'm just trying to protect myself. You have someone barge in your house in the middle of the night and accuse you of all sorts of things and then see how anxious you are to get personal with someone you're working with."

"I like the way your hair in the back curls."

"I think we should keep things—"

"I like your strong, rugged jaw."

"—low-key and professional."

"I like your thick eyebrows. It's like two small forests. And I love your voice. You sound like that guy on the radio—what's his name? Tom Bodett, isn't it? 'We'll leave a light on.' You'd leave a light on for me, wouldn't you, Ben?"

For just a second they found themselves staring at each other. He panicked, stood up, and started pacing the floor. "Well, okay, we're finished with that. Now let's get to work. We need to decide where we're going to practice."

"How about right here? Nobody ever uses this room anyway."

"You think it would be okay with your parents?"

"I'm sure it will, but I'll ask my dad."

"I hope I get to meet your dad sometime."

"I hope so too. He's been really busy lately at work. We don't see much of him around here anymore."

"I wondered about that. I saw a bunch of things upstairs that need fixing, you know, things that fathers do on Saturdays. Growing up in the hardware business, I notice things like that."

"Like what?"

"When I washed up for supper, I noticed you have a leaky faucet in the bathroom. And in the kitchen one of the chairs

14

is wobbly. If you want, I can do some repair work after we finish over the next few days."

"My mom would love that. She'll probably want you to stay for supper all the time if you start fixing things around here."

"Sure, no problem. That's what I liked most when I worked for my dad, being able to help people."

"My dad gets around to things like that eventually, but right now he's so busy that . . . " She paused. "He doesn't have time for us."

They practiced Wednesday and Thursday, working up what he thought would be enough songs for Friday and Saturday at Angelo's.

Ben knew they sounded good but wasn't sure if anyone else would notice. Before, when he and Julia sang at the restaurant, people either ignored them or else just stared at them while eating their pizzas. Ben wondered if people knew how strange they looked with cheese dangling from their chins.

On Friday night at Angelo's it was even better than Ben thought it would be. The two of them together had a fresh, new, vibrant sound. Not only that, but for every song they sang, Kimberly acted as if the song had been personally written for her. When they finished all the songs they'd practiced, people started calling for more. "What are we going to do? We don't have any more songs," Kimberly said.

"Let's do your graduation song the way we changed it."

The crowd loved it.

After they finished, Angelo Postrollo, the manager, came up and treated them like they were part of the family. He gave them a pizza to eat while they waited for their next show.

A man came over to their table. "Do you have any tapes of your music for sale?"

"No, not yet, but we will soon. We're working on it," Ben said.

15

Three other people came up and told them they liked their music.

"We could've made an extra fifty dollars tonight if we'd had the tapes to sell," Ben said.

"Okay, I'll give you an extra half hour a day, but that's all I can do, or I'll end up flunking everything."

On the way home that night, he had a difficult time bringing up what was bothering him, but finally he decided to just start. "You're really a good actor," he said.

"How do you mean?"

"On some of the love songs, the way you looked at me, I mean, it was very effective."

She snickered. "Yes, I could tell that—you missed two entrances."

"Yeah, sorry. See, the thing is, Julia and I didn't interact much that way. We just stood up there and sang."

"Must've been pretty boring for the audience, right?"

His shoulders slumped. "Yeah, it was."

"What are you saying, Ben?"

"I don't know. I've never had a girl look at me the way you did tonight."

"I'm just trying to give the folks a good show. Relax, okay? You're safe with me. You're not the only guy in my life. I mean, like, Sunday I'm seeing a guy I used to go with in high school. He just got out of prison but he's really a nice guy. He just made one little mistake."

Ben felt a panic attack coming on. "What kind of mistake?"

"He knifed a guy he caught talking to me in the hallway. We've been writing all the time he's been in jail. I told him about you, and he seemed really interested. He even asked where you live." She looked at his reaction, then burst out laughing. "Just kidding, okay?"

"Don't ever do that again."

"I know, I know. Low-key and professional, that's my middle name."

They got together every day at four o'clock and either practiced or wrote songs. Ben was often asked to stay for supper. After they finished eating, while Kimberly studied, he sometimes did repair work around the house. And then around eight he went to his apartment to study.

Having Ben around the house was all right with Derek. He enjoyed having another guy to talk to. Megan also basked in the attention Ben gave her.

Paul Madison, the father of the family, often worked late at his office. When he did come home in time for supper, Ben couldn't help but compare him to his own father. Paul Madison was younger looking than his wife, but as time passed the achievement was taking considerable effort. He seemed obsessed with reducing the fat content of the food he ate. He never had dessert, avoided eating much meat, and didn't even put butter or margarine on the half slice of bread he might have with his meal. Ben couldn't help but wonder whom he was trying to impress.

In contrast, Ben's father, who treated his employees to sweet rolls every morning at the hardware store, had put on several extra pounds over the last few years.

In the home where Ben grew up, after supper his father helped with dishes. It gave his folks time to talk about what had happened during the day. But in Kimberly's family, their father seemed to have very little to do with his wife either before or after supper.

Ben could see there was tension in the family, but he didn't worry about it much because he had learned from his mission that almost every family has a few problems.

One afternoon a week later, Kimberly and Ben were in her father's office in the basement. They had the door closed so the electric heater in the room could keep them warm.

Kimberly's mother, Anne, had just come home from shopping for groceries. They could hear her asking Derek to help her unload the groceries from the car. A minute later she came downstairs to put another load into the washing machine. She must not have realized Kimberly and Ben were in the office writing out a final version of a song they had just composed.

Paul Madison came downstairs. "I'm home but I have to go back again tonight," Ben heard him say.

"Is business that good that you have to be gone four nights a week?" Anne asked.

"You know how it is this time of year."

"Does Gloria work with you when you work nights?"

"Not usually. Why do you ask?"

"Just curious." A long pause. "I took Megan to the dentist today. He says she needs braces."

"How much will that cost?"

"Around three thousand dollars," she said.

"We can't afford it."

"People can never afford braces. It's something parents have to do, one way or the other."

"Maybe she'll grow out of it," he said.

"Look, you're welcome to talk to the dentist yourself."

"What did you tell him?"

"I said I'd get back to him after I talked to you."

"I need some time to figure out where the money's coming from. Let's put it on hold for a while."

"We can't wait too long."

"I know that. What else do we need to talk about?"

"Can you talk to Derek about finishing up his Eagle project?"

"I thought he was working on it."

"He was but it's hard for him. He could use your help in mapping out what he needs to do."

"Can't you do that?"

"Yes, but I think you should. It would give you a reason to spend some time around here. You're never here anymore."

"You know what work is like for me this time of year."

18

"It's not so much the time you're away. You always work hard, but this year for some reason it's different. Now it's like you're not a part of the family anymore."

"If you want, I'll talk to the dentist about Megan's braces."

After her parents went back up the stairs, Kimberly was silent for a long time. Then she said, "Most of the time my mom and dad get along okay. I guess it's just that he hasn't been home much lately."

"Sure," Ben said, but at the same time he couldn't help but notice how worried Kimberly looked.

2

During supper a week later, Megan was excited because her dad was taking her to the Ice Capades. He wasn't home yet, but he'd promised to pick her up at seven-thirty in order to get there for an eight o'clock performance.

Ben ate supper with the family and then stayed to fix a dripping faucet in the bathroom on the first floor. What should have been a five-minute job was turning into a major project because the faucet was so old. Ben finally suggested to Kimberly's mother that she buy a washerless faucet. She agreed. So after another trip to the hardware store, he was on his back with his head in the bathroom cabinet under the faucet. Kimberly was sitting cross-legged on the floor in jeans and sweatshirt, trying to keep him company while studying chemistry at the same time.

"How's it going?" she asked after hearing him grumble.

"Ever wonder why there's so few happy plumbers?"

"That bad, huh?"

"I've seen worse."

"What a guy. My mom really appreciates this. Last night she told me, 'Any guy can take you to a movie, but a guy who can fix things around the house is worth his weight in gold.'"

A few minutes after seven, Megan stuck her head in the bathroom.

"Use the bathroom upstairs," Kimberly said.

20

"I know. I just want to talk to Ben for a while."

"Hi, Megan!" Ben called out, his head and shoulders still inside the cabinet.

"What are you doing in there?"

"Replacing the faucet."

"Is that hard?"

"Not once I get the old one out." Ben scooted out long enough to get a good look at Megan. The turquoise in her sweater somehow made her eyes come alive. He was certain she had no idea how terrific she looked. "You all ready for your daddy-daughter date?"

"I've been ready for ten minutes. The show starts at eight. I want to be there before it begins. I hate to be late to things."

"Your dad will probably show up any minute now."

"He said he'd be here by seven-fifteen."

"There," Ben said, "the rest will be easy." He slid out, stood up, and lifted out the old faucet.

"I need to phone somebody about an assignment," Kimberly said. "Megan, will you keep Ben company?"

"Sure."

Kimberly left.

"You've got a smudge on your face," Megan said. She got a tissue and wiped his cheek.

"Thank you."

"We have to keep you looking good for Kimberly."

"We do? Why?"

"She talks about you all the time."

"She does?"

"Of course. One night she even dreamed about you."

"Oh? Tell me about it." He tried to sound only mildly interested, but he wanted to know every detail of Kimberly's dream. His heart started beating faster, and he felt as if the room had suddenly become too warm.

"She didn't tell me any of the details, but she did say it was very romantic."

21

He was glad his head was in the cabinet so Megan wouldn't know how red his face was.

Megan went to the kitchen to check on the time and then came back. "How long does it take to get downtown?"

"I don't know—fifteen minutes, I guess."

"If my dad gets here soon, we can still make it in time."

"Sure. Look, Megan, if for some reason your dad doesn't come, as soon as I get this fixed, I'll take you out for ice cream."

"You and Kimberly, you mean."

"No, Kimberly's got to study. Just you and me."

"I'd rather go out with my dad than with you."

"Of course. And he'll be here any second too, I just know he will."

Megan got a kitchen chair and set it in the doorway and watched him work. "This isn't the first time he's been late."

"He's not late now."

"No, not really—he's just later than he said he'd be." She paused. "If he were taking Kimberly, he'd be on time."

"He's not doing this on purpose. Something probably came up."

"I know." She stood up and looked in the mirror. "Do I look okay?"

"You look great. I mean it. Sometimes I wish I was your same age so I could grow up with you. Then we could be friends together in school."

"You're crazy then. Growing up once is bad enough. I'd never want to do it twice."

As the minutes slipped by, Megan quit talking.

"How you doing there, kiddo?" he asked.

"I guess we'll miss the beginning, but that's okay. It's two hours long, so there's plenty to see even if we are a little late."

"If your dad doesn't come, we can go see if they have any tickets left, and if they do, I'll take you."

"No. The main reason I wanted to go was because my dad

asked me." There was a long pause, and then she said, "He doesn't really care that much for me anyway."

"Of course he does."

She didn't answer except to say, several minutes later, "I guess he's not coming. I'm going to go up and change and then finish my homework." She left.

A few minutes later Kimberly returned. "How's it going?"

"You'd better go talk to Megan. She's pretty disappointed."

"I know. I just talked to her. Poor kid."

A short time later Paul Madison burst into the house. "Where's Megan? Is she ready?"

"Megan, your father's here!" Anne called out.

Megan came to the second-floor railing and called out, "Just a minute, Daddy, I need to change back to what I was wearing."

"Paul, could I talk with you in here?" Anne asked her husband.

They went into their bedroom, next to the bathroom where Ben was working. The bathroom had two entrances, one from the hall and one from the master bedroom. The door to the hall was open but the door to the master bedroom was shut.

"Where on earth have you been?" he could hear Anne saying. "You told Megan you'd pick her up at seven-fifteen. It's now five minutes to eight. Why do you do this to me and the children time after time?"

Kimberly and Ben could hear what was being said, even through the closed door. Ben continued to work, hoping he could finish and get out before things got too bad.

"I don't do this all the time," Paul said.

"You can take me for granted if you want, but I won't have you taking your children for granted."

"I'm not taking anybody for granted," Paul said. He opened the door to the bathroom from the master bedroom and saw Ben and Kimberly sitting on the floor and the old faucet as well as several tools scattered about. He turned to Anne. "Excuse me, but what is going on here?"

"I asked Ben to fix the leak," Anne said.

"To fix a leak, you don't need a whole new faucet."

Ben tried to explain. "Everything was so old and . . . uh . . . well . . . your wife said it kept leaking even after you fixed it, so I thought it'd be better to get a good washerless faucet. Now you won't be bothered by it anymore."

"Listen to me," Paul lectured Ben, "I want you to put everything back the way it was, take the new faucet back to the store, and get your money back. I'm not paying for a new faucet when the old one is perfectly good."

Megan came to the bathroom entrance. "Hi, Daddy, when are we leaving?"

"In just a minute, sweetheart. Go get in the car."

Megan went out to the car.

"My gosh," Anne said, "aren't you even going to apologize to your daughter for being late?"

"I'll take care of it when I'm in the car. What I want to know is who told Ben he could buy a new faucet."

"I did," Anne said.

"Why on earth would you do something like that?"

"How long have I been after you to fix that faucet? Well, it got so bad I couldn't wait any longer. Ben said he'd do it. He suggested we get the kind that doesn't need a washer."

"I realize you don't understand things like this, but I can guarantee that what he's done is a total waste of money. I'm having him pack it all up and take it back."

"You're not doing anything of the kind! That boy has been working on this for over an hour, and you don't have the decency to thank him for trying to help out. He knows what he's doing, and he's willing to do it as a favor to us. When you come back, there will be a new faucet in the bathroom, and that's all there is to it. Now go so you don't miss any more of the show. I mean, it would be nice if you could get there before intermission. If you could have seen how excited Megan was to be going out with her dad and then see how hurt she got as the time passed and you didn't show up. What were you doing that was more important than being on time for your daughter? Now I'm sure you think you can go out there and turn on your charm and sweet-talk her out of her disappointment, but it doesn't work that way. If you were going to be late, why didn't you at least call?"

Paul turned and, without another word, walked out.

The storm was over, but Ben felt exhausted by the tension he'd felt. He picked up his tools and put them back in the tool chest. After turning on the new faucet and letting cold water flow, he sat down to check underneath to make sure there were no leaks.

Kimberly came up from behind, knelt down, and gave him a hug. "Hey, Mister Fix-It Man, I think you're wonderful."

"You do? Thanks."

"I'm really sorry you got put in the middle of this."

"No problem."

She stood up. "I hope Megan has a good time tonight, don't you? It didn't start out very well, but maybe it'll get better once they get there."

"I bet it will."

Anne came in. "You're all done?"

"Sure." He turned the water on and off a couple of times.

"Oh, would you look at that!" Anne exclaimed. "No more leaky faucets. How wonderful! Thank you so much."

"Hey, it's the least I can do for all the meals you've been feeding me lately."

"We enjoy having you here," Anne said. "Ben, I need to apologize for my husband. He's under a lot of pressure at work right now. I'm sure that once things calm down, he'll be really grateful for all you've done for us tonight."

"If he won't pay for the new faucet, I will," he said.

"Thanks for offering, but that won't be necessary."

*   *   *   *   *

25

Ben lived in an upstairs apartment in his aunt's house. She had been happily married for twenty-five years, and then four years ago her husband suddenly had a heart attack and died. He sat in his aunt's kitchen that night and told her what had happened at Kimberly's. They stayed up late and talked about marriage and families and the problems that come into people's lives.

3

A few days later Ben phoned Kimberly. "I've got a way for us to make some extra money next Friday night, if you're interested," he said.

She laughed. "Excuse me, but did you say extra money?"

"You'd better hear what it is before you decide. My dad's store is having its annual banquet, and they have some money budgeted for entertainment. My mom just called to ask if we'd be interested in singing. We could drive to Rock Springs Friday afternoon, go to the banquet and perform, then stay the night at my folks' place. We'll come back Saturday and work for Angelo that night. My dad's store will pay us each two hundred dollars. I think it's mainly because my mom wishes I'd come home more often. What do you think?"

"What's Angelo going to say?"

"I already talked to him. He says it's okay. His nephew has a group and keeps bugging Angelo to let them play at the restaurant. It'll work out okay, if you're interested."

"Let's do it," she said.

"Okay, I'll tell them they can count on us." He paused. "Now there's just one thing. You're the first girl I've taken home to meet my parents since my mission. They're both trying to get me married off. If my mom thinks there's anything going on between us, she'll ask if we need any help picking out wedding invitations."

"Well, we'll be honest and let her know we're just friends."

"Honesty? That might work with some parents, but I'm not sure it will with mine."

On Friday afternoon at four-thirty they arrived at his home in Rock Springs. They came with a plan. "Mom, this is, uh, oh gosh, I forgot your name."

"Kimberly."

"Yeah, right, Kimberly . . . Mitchell?"

"It's Madison, actually," Kimberly said.

"Oh yeah, right, Kimberly Madison. She'll be playing guitar and singing with me tonight."

"Kimberly, I'm very happy to meet you. Ben didn't tell me how lovely you are," his mother said.

His father, a big man with a booming voice, gave Kimberly a big hug. He was still wearing his red Ace Hardware vest from work, a vest he hadn't been able to button for years.

"Uh, Kathryn, would you like me to show you to your room?" Ben asked.

"It's Kimberly!" her father and mother both said at the same time.

"Yeah, right. Gosh, I don't know why I can't remember your name."

He carried her suitcase to the guest bedroom. "The bathroom is across the hall. Knowing my mom, there's probably some guest towels on the counter in there. If you need extra blankets during the night, there's some in the closet. I think that's all I'm supposed to say. Anything you need, just let us know."

The banquet was held in the dining hall of a motel. When they entered the room, there was a banner on the wall that read, "Welcome Ace Hardware Employees." They sat at a round table near the front of the hall.

"What are you studying in college?" Mr. Fairbanks asked Kimberly.

"History," Ben answered for her.

28

"No, not history," she said. "I'm majoring in mechanical engineering."

"Oh, right," Ben said. "Another girl I spend time with is majoring in history. It's hard to keep it all straight."

The show they presented was well received. They sang songs the audience would be familiar with, but the last song they sang was the one they'd worked on the first time they got together, her graduation song. When they finished, several in the crowd stood up and shouted their approval. They were asked to do an encore. They did two more songs they'd written together. After they finished, people came up and told them how much they enjoyed the program. And then a country western band started setting up. Ben and Kimberly stayed for a couple of dances and then decided to go back to Ben's house.

When they got there, Ben started a fire in the fireplace while Kimberly fixed them some hot chocolate. It was a cold February night, and the wind was drifting snow across the road they'd just traveled over.

Ben turned off all the lights in the house except the one in the kitchen. They sat in front of the fire and talked and sipped hot chocolate and ate cookies. His fingers picked out snatches of new songs on the guitar while they talked.

"Your parents seem to get along really well," she said.

"Yeah, I guess they do. They argue sometimes, but they're always able to work things out."

"I like them a lot. I can see now why you turned out the way you did. You got your love of music from your mom and your down-to-earth practicality from your dad."

"I never thought about it before, but you're probably right. My mom was the one who made sure I had music lessons when I was a kid. In high school I played trumpet in band, and I was in choir too. My parents always went to our concerts — my mom because she loved music, my dad mainly because I was in it."

"When did you learn to play guitar?" she asked.

"The year after I graduated from high school, while I was working for my dad and saving for a mission." He put another log on the fire. "What do you want to do now? Watch a movie? Play a video game?"

"Oh, let's just talk," she said. "There's a lot about you I don't know, even though we do get together every day."

"It's just that when we're together we have more important things to do. My time with you is the most important part of my day."

"Because of the music, right?"

"Yeah, sure."

"Have you ever been in love?" she asked.

She was sitting close enough to him that it seemed natural for him to put his arm around her shoulder. "In high school I was," he said.

"What happened?"

"I went on a mission. When I came back, she was married. What about you?"

"Not really. Actually, I have no business writing songs about love when I've never experienced it firsthand."

"You do okay."

"For some people this'd be a romantic situation, the two of us sitting in front of a fire, a snowstorm outside, just the two of us here alone with the lights down low."

"A snowy night, a fireplace, the shadows from a fire upon your face."

She set her hot chocolate down just in case he was about to kiss her.

He paused. " 'A snowy night, a fireplace, the shadows from a fire upon your face.' What do you think? It might work. Get your guitar. Let's see if we can get a song out of this. Or how about this—'A fireplace hearth on a winter night, your face aglow in the firelight.' "

She moved away. "Do we have to do this now? Why can't we watch TV or pop popcorn or do what ordinary people do?"

"I'm sorry. You're right. We need to forget about music for a while. You want to watch a movie?"

"No, not really. I probably should study a little. I've got a chemistry test Monday."

"Yeah, sure, go ahead. You can use the kitchen table if you want. I'll see if I can come up with another song for our tape. Oh, I talked to a friend of mine who has a friend whose uncle has a recording studio in Provo. If we can get with him some night, he'll record all our songs for us for practically nothing. I was thinking about next Friday after we get done at Angelo's. Will that work for you?"

"Yes, I think so."

"Good."

She laid her books on the kitchen table. He sat by the fire with his guitar in his hand, hunting for the rest of the melody and words to the song they would later call "Winter Love."

When he had a first version finished, he went into the kitchen and sang it to her. She adored the sound of his voice. While he was singing, she looked up at him, and for a brief instant, low-key and professional was thrown out, and they were looking at each other like two people in love.

When he finished, they were still staring at each other. "What do you think?" he asked, sounding like he was under a magical spell.

"About what?" she asked.

"I don't know."

"Me neither."

"What's going on?" he asked.

"I don't know."

"Me neither, but something is."

"Yes."

He thought about kissing her, but she was sitting down holding a calculator and he was standing up with a guitar in his hand. It would be a little awkward.

They heard his parents pull into the driveway. Instinctively,

31

she returned to her book and he went into the living room and turned on more lights.

"Hey, you two! Everyone is still talking about how wonderful you sounded together tonight," his mother bubbled as she came in.

"Yes. Everyone told me how much they enjoyed your program," his dad echoed.

His parents challenged Ben and Kimberly to a game of Pictionary. They sat around the kitchen table and played and ate popcorn and laughed and teased each other and gloated when they guessed right.

For Kimberly, along with the fun was a sadness that came from the realization that her parents had long ago quit playing board games on the kitchen table with the family. She felt like she needed to be alone, so she excused herself and went to her room to get ready for bed.

"She's a fine girl," she heard Mr. Fairbanks say as she walked down the hall to the guest room. It was easy to hear him anywhere in the house.

"I know that," Ben said.

"She'd make a good wife."

"I know that too."

"Then what's the problem?"

"We just work together."

"You can say anything you want," Mrs. Fairbanks said, "but when you were up there singing, everyone noticed the way you were staring at each other. I'm sure of one thing—it's not just business with her. And I don't think it is with you either."

"No, not really, but we're trying not to rush into anything. You know the mess I had with Julia and that guy she was going with. I don't want to repeat that again. And besides, I wish I could explain what it's like when we work together writing music. It's magic. I'm afraid of losing that. I think we have a real shot at making it big."

"If you make it big, fine," his father said, "but don't sacrifice your education for some one-in-a-million chance that most likely won't pan out anyway. I'll tell you one thing. There's a lot more hardware store owners and also people with business degrees making it than there are singers and guitar pickers. You get your education first and then worry about this 'making it big' foolishness later."

"Yeah, right. Look, I think I'll go to bed now."

"Let's have family prayer," his mother said.

After family prayer, his father said, "Oh, one thing, the roads are getting worse. You might think about staying until this storm blows over."

"I'll see how it is in the morning."

"I was hoping you'd stay until Sunday after church," his mother said.

"Sorry, Mom, we've got to get back. We're supposed to work at Angelo's tomorrow night."

Kimberly lay in bed wide awake. She heard Ben go down the hall to his room. She realized she was falling in love for the very first time. On the way up from Utah, while he drove, she had studied his face. She could close her eyes now and bring it again to mind—his thick, sandy-colored hair that seemed impossible to muss up (she called it industrial-strength hair), the small, nearly invisible scar on his right cheek caused by a bicycle accident when he was twelve, his long face with prominent cheekbones that somehow reminded her (although she never told him) of a young, beardless, and still cheerful Abraham Lincoln.

His parents finished the leftover hot chocolate. When they passed the guest bedroom on their way down the hall to their room, they danced to the out-of-tune humming of Mr. Fairbanks. "This is our night, kiddo," he said as softly as he could, but with his gravelly voice, he could be heard in every room in the house.

"Is that right?" she teased.

"Absolutely."

They danced into their bedroom and closed the door.

Kimberly started to cry. She was really worried about her parents.

After breakfast Ben and Kimberly said good-bye to his mother and then drove to the hardware store to see his dad.

Ben gave her a tour of the store, which was crammed with merchandise of every kind. A tall girl in her early twenties, with short brown hair and a mischievous smile, breezed past them. She was wearing jeans, a long-sleeved wool shirt, and an Ace Hardware vest. "Better not let the boss catch you making out on company time," she teased Ben as she led a customer to where they kept the axe handles.

"That's Jeni," Ben said. "She's a walking hardware encyclopedia. Anything I can do, she can do better."

Jeni returned a minute later. "Hey, you two, except for the fact it wasn't country western, your singing last night wasn't half bad. Of course, it could've been a lot better," she said, with a broad smile in Ben's direction.

"How could it have been better, Jeni? Please, won't you tell me?" he asked, knowing full well what was coming.

"It would've been better if we hadn't been able to hear you."

"Yeah, yeah. Kimberly, this is Jeni. She's lean and mean, but people come for miles around to ask her advice on how to fix things."

"Hey, somebody around here has to know what's going on. It's for sure Ben doesn't. The only reason he can get a job here every summer is because he's the boss's son."

"That's right, and don't you ever forget it."

"How can I? You bring it up every ten minutes," Jeni said. "Well, not everyone around here can stand around and make eyes at their sweetie. I guess I'd better get back to work."

"Whoa! Did you say you're actually going to work? Wait, let me get my camera."

"Careful, Ben, don't get me riled. Did I ever tell you about the time we put a paper towel in Mel's bologna sandwich? He never even noticed. This summer if your dad makes a mistake and hires you again, you'd better check your lunches. Fair warning." She left to go help another customer.

"As you can see, Jeni and I have this thing going."

"You really like it here, don't you," Kimberly said. It was more of a statement than a question.

"Oh, yeah. This is my second home. This is where I learned to work and where I found out I like serving the customer."

"And that's why you're majoring in business?"

"I think so."

"Are you going to come back and work here after you graduate?"

"I might. It's not a bad life. Our customers are like old friends. For almost anything that breaks down in this town, we're the first ones to know about it. You're probably not impressed by shelves full of bolts and nails, but it's important to the people around here. There's something I've been thinking about lately though. Stores like this are dying out. Before long there won't be people around like Mel or Jeni. I'm wondering if there's a way to use technology so that a customer can have the advantage of talking to someone who can answer their questions. Some sort of a computer data base with all sorts of practical hints. Right now it's just in the dreaming stage." He looked at his watch. "Well, I guess we'd better tell my dad good-bye and then take off."

They found his father helping a man with a bad back decide what kind of snow shovel would be best for him to get. When the man decided and left, Ben said, "Dad, we're going to take off now."

"Have you checked the weather report?"

"Yes."

"And?"

"I think we can make it."

"Famous last words," his father said, resting his large hand on Ben's shoulder. "Look, son, you be careful, and if there's any problem, let us know right away. You got that?"

"Okay, sure."

Mr. Fairbanks turned to Kimberly. "It was an honor for us to have you come visit us. You look like an angel and you sing like one too. Now you make sure Ben doesn't do anything stupid out on that highway." He gave her a hug.

They started to leave.

"Oh, one more thing, there's still some donuts and rolls in the back if you want to take 'em along," his father called out.

"Thanks, Dad, we'll grab a couple on our way out."

They left Rock Springs at eleven in the morning. Though it was still snowing, the wind had died down and the interstate was still open. But the farther they drove, the worse it got. The wind picked up and started laying down drifts across the road. Just before they reached Green River, there was a state highway patrol car parked across the road. The officer told them that the interstate was closed and they should go into Green River and wait out the storm.

"How long will that be?" Ben asked.

"Around here you never know. It could be a couple of days or just a few hours."

"Where do people go while they're waiting?"

"There's probably still some motel rooms in town, but they'll be going fast."

Ben glanced over in Kimberly's direction, then said, "We're not in the market for a motel room."

"Try the high school then. They'll be putting people up during the storm."

They were among the first ones at the high school. They were each assigned an army cot and a blanket.

They decided on a place to set up their temporary home, then phoned their parents and told them where they were. Ben asked his parents to call Angelo and tell him they weren't going to make it that night. Next they found a store and stocked up on junk food. Then they returned to the gym.

They sat on the floor through the long afternoon with an army blanket wrapped around them and watched people file in, truckers unhappy about being shut down, families with children who cried, salesmen unlucky to have been caught on the road during a blizzard.

At seven that night Ben went to his car, got his guitar, and came back in and started playing some songs. Children drifted over to where he was. He taught them several songs and had them sing with him. Then he did silly songs and monster imitations that made the kids shriek. He wrestled with them, carried them on his back, and made them giggle and laugh and beg for more. They clung to his back, wrapped their arms around his legs, tried to tickle him, came up and hugged him. One little boy even fell asleep on his blanket.

And then a woman in a fur coat came over and told him the children were creating too much of a commotion and that Ben was the worst of all. He was told to act his age and let the children calm down so they'd be able to sleep that night.

It was all over. Parents came and took their children, and Ben was forced to turn into an adult again.

"Just when I make up my mind not to like you, you do something wonderful," Kimberly said.

He smiled. "Let's face it, life is unfair."

"How did you get all those kids to love you?"

"I guess there's a part of me that never grew up."

They lay on separate cots, next to each other. They listened to the combined noises of sixty people around them coughing, talking, trying to get to sleep. Somewhere in the dim light a man was snoring loudly.

"It's going to be a long night," she said quietly.

37

"At least we're together and can talk."

"Remember in kindergarten when you used to take naps in the middle of the day," she said, " and it didn't matter if a girl or a boy was next to you on the floor. Everyone was the same. That's what this reminds me of."

"I wished I'd been in kindergarten with you," he said.

"Why?" she teased. "So we could write songs without that dreaded physical attraction getting in the way?"

"I just wish I'd known you then," he said. "I bet you were a cute kid."

"Of course I was."

"Are you going to dream about me tonight?" he asked.

She sat up. "Who told you about that?"

"Megan."

"What did she say?"

"She told me you had a romantic dream about me. This might be a good time for you to tell me all about it."

"No, go away."

"C'mon, why not? I like bedtime stories."

"It would be too embarrassing."

"Now you've really got my interest."

"Quit talking and let me get to sleep." She turned her back to him, a signal she was through talking for the night.

Strangely enough, he dreamed about her that night. It made him realize how much he cared for her. But also, like her, he didn't want to tell her about his dream either.

In the morning Ben was the first to wake up. Kimberly was facing him but still asleep. It gave him an opportunity to look at her. Her face was relaxed, her breathing slow and even.

She woke up. "Have you been watching me sleep?" she asked.

"Yes."

"Just shows how desperate a person can get when there's no TV."

"I'm not complaining."

The road didn't open until one o'clock in the afternoon. And then they were on their way.

"I've been thinking that we both need a little romance in our lives," he said. "So I think we should concentrate on dating after we finish at Angelo's on the weekends."

She was surprised, but delighted. "You do?"

"Yes. If you need any help, I know some guys I can line you up with, so then we can keep working."

Her smile vanished. "Who will you date?"

"Don't worry about me. I've got plenty of girls to choose from. What about you?"

"Same thing with me," she said. "I turn down dates all the time."

"I didn't know that."

"Oh yes, all the time."

From the way she looked at him, he knew she was disappointed, but he didn't know what else to do.

4

The next Friday night after they finished at Angelo's, Ben and Kimberly recorded all their songs at a recording studio belonging to an uncle of a friend of a friend's. It took them until three in the morning before they finally finished. But when they listened to the tape again on Monday, they decided it was worth it.

They duplicated one hundred tapes and put handmade labels on them. At Angelo's the next week they sold four tapes. To them it was sweet success.

On their Wyoming trip Kimberly and Ben had come to an understanding about dating others, which in the beginning made sense but within two weeks had degenerated into a bizarre game.

"I had the most wonderful date last night," Ben said as he stared into Kimberly's eyes during one of their afternoon practices.

"Tell me all about it," she said.

"Her name is Courtney Thomas. She's a model. She's done three covers for *Seventeen*. She's a returned missionary. She speaks three languages. She's majoring in Russian studies too. She's away a lot because when any Russian dignitary comes to the West Coast, they hire her to act as a translator. She's writing a book about foreign policy. The book's going to be published next fall. In her spare time she teaches aerobics and works with the elderly. I couldn't believe how well we got along together. For some reason she was really attracted to me."

"How could you tell?"

"Well, when we were in the theater, she leaned her head on my shoulder and reached out for my hand."

"You mean like this?" Kimberly said, repeating the action.

"Yes, like that."

"How did that make you feel?"

"Well, I felt like she must like me a lot. I think she and I are about to become romantically involved."

"I'm so happy for you. I've also found someone to become romantically involved with. His name is Christopher Monti-leaux. He's a returned missionary. He plays first-chair violin for the Utah Symphony, and he's also a member of the Olympic ski team. He was here with the team this weekend. They were driving by when he saw me downtown. He told the driver to stop, and then he got out and ran up to me. We spent the rest of the day together. So now I too am romantically involved with a wonderful person."

"We're very lucky to both be romantically involved," Ben said.

"Yes, very. Did you kiss Courtney?"

"No. She begged me to kiss her, but I told her it wasn't right on the first date."

"That was very wise."

"Have you kissed what's his name?"

She stood up. "No, but once when he was practicing his violin, I came up behind him like this . . . and put my arms around his neck like this . . . and bent over and blew into his ear like this . . . and asked him how his practicing was going."

"That must have melted his violin."

"Just the rosin."

"We're very fortunate to both be romantically involved," he said.

41

"Yes, we are."

He kissed her. It was not the first time. The last few times they'd gotten together in the basement to learn some new songs, they'd ended up kissing. The only problem was that outside of that room they pretended it had never happened.

This time was different. She held up her hand. "Time out." She brushed back strands of hair. "Look, whatever happened to low-key and professional?"

"Oh, that. Good question."

"We're supposed to be working now, not doing this."

"I know. Sorry. Any suggestions?" he asked.

"I think we need to be honest with each other and face the fact that we have feelings for one another and, no matter how much we try to deny it, they're not going to go away. No more making up people, okay?"

"All right," he said.

"We have to make a separation between working and . . . uh . . . recreation or whatever you call what we were just doing."

"We were kissing."

"Yes, that's right, we were. And another thing. You've got to give me more time to study. I think we should practice from four to five and then you should go back to your aunt's place. We're spending too much time together. I can't study about chemical reactions when you're trying to braid my hair at the same time, because that causes plenty of chemical reactions in me. Also, we can't keep practicing down here in the basement, because it's too isolated. We need to get upstairs where we'll be bothered. We could practice upstairs in the hallway. There's always someone going by there."

They moved their chairs and guitars and music stand to the hallway upstairs.

"What's going on?" Derek asked.

"We're going to work up here for a while."

"What for?"

"Ambience," Kimberly said.

"I don't know what that word means," Derek said.

"That's why I used it," Kimberly said.

"And people say *I'm* weird."

After they finished practicing, Kimberly said, "Go home now, Ben."

A few minutes later, though, they were still lingering at the doorway.

"What happens now?" he asked.

"If you want us to get together socially, then you ask me out. That's how it's done in the real world. Why should we be any different?"

"Look, I'm sorry about how this has turned out. I owe you an apology," he said. "This is what I was trying to avoid by talking about low-key and professional. Guess I didn't do a very good job, did I?"

"It's not totally your fault," she said. "It was just something that happened. But we've got to make a separation or we'll ruin everything—both the singing and our relationship."

"So we're entering a new phase then, is that it?" he asked.

"Yes, that's what it is, a new phase. Good day, sir."

"Will you go out with me this weekend?"

"I'd like that very much."

"Good. It's a deal then. It's a pleasure being professional with you." He shook her hand, wished he could kiss her again, decided against it, and then left.

5

A few days later Kimberly came home early to clean the house before Ben showed up. She hung up her coat. "I'm home!" she called out. No answer. She entered the kitchen but nobody was there. She could hear Derek's video game in the TV room, so she went in to see him. "Where's Mom?" she asked.

"She's in her room. She's got a headache." Derek sounded relieved not to be hassled about after-school chores. "You're supposed to go see her. What I want to know is, who's fixing supper?"

"Is feeding your stomach the only thing you can think about?"

"I'm sorry she's sick, all right? But I'm also hungry."

"Have you done your after-school jobs?" Kimberly asked.

"You're not my mother," he said.

"It won't kill you to help out once in a while. We don't want Dad coming home to a messy house again."

"It doesn't matter. He never comes home anyway," he said.

"This is a busy time of year for him."

"Shut the door when you leave, okay?"

Kimberly knew her mother probably wanted her to fix supper, so she decided to change clothes first. When she entered her bedroom, she found Megan standing in front of the mirror wearing a sweater Kimberly had received last Christmas. "Caught you, didn't I?"

Megan looked at her but didn't smile. "Something's wrong," she said.

"I know. Mom's not feeling well. Derek told me."

"It's more than that. You go talk to her. She always tells you things."

"Okay. What do you have in mind for that sweater of mine?"

"Nothing. I was just trying on some of your things. I wish I was like you."

"Whatever for?"

"People pay attention to you."

"They pay attention to you too."

"Not really. We were reading out loud today in English, and it talked about someone being a plain-looking girl, and I heard one of the guys whisper, 'Yeah, like Megan.' "

"Don't pay attention to guys like that. I'll tell you one thing—I wish I had your face. It's so perfect. I mean it."

"You're just saying that."

Kimberly took Megan's face in her hands and leaned until their foreheads were nearly touching. With each word, she gently bumped her forehead to Megan's. "I . . . love . . . your . . . face."

"Nobody knows I'm even alive," Megan said.

"That's not true."

"It is."

"Don't you know how wonderful you are?"

"I'm not anything."

"I won't listen to you talking like this. Besides, we've got to start supper before Dad gets home. We'll talk later. But look, if you want to wear my sweater tomorrow, go ahead. It's a little big for you but not too bad. Just don't spill anything on it."

Kimberly changed, then went downstairs to her mother's bedroom. She knocked on the door, and her mother told her to come in. "Derek and Megan say you're not feeling well," Kimberly said as she entered. "You want me to fix supper?"

Her mother sat up in bed. "That would be a big help."

"What do you want me to fix?"

"I thought we'd have spaghetti. There's hamburger in the refrigerator you can cook, and some bottles of spaghetti sauce in the storeroom. If you're going to have Ben stay for supper, make a little extra."

"He won't be staying for supper anymore."

"Why not?"

"We just work on music together, that's all. Well, I guess I'd better fix supper before Derek starts chewing on the furniture."

"Don't fix anything for your father. He won't be coming home for supper."

"Is he working late again?"

Her mother didn't answer. Kimberly thought maybe she hadn't heard the question and was about to leave when her mother said, "I don't know what to say about your father."

"What do you mean?"

"He's found someone else."

The only thing Kimberly could think of about her father finding someone else was the time her father had brought home a kitten he'd found near his office. They'd kept it; it was still in the family. To Kimberly it would have made more sense if her mother had said her father had found another kitten or another animal, but saying he had found someone else didn't make any sense at all. "I don't understand."

"Today he told me he wants a divorce."

In the bleak darkness of the room Kimberly heard the muffled sounds from the TV. She tried to imagine that in the TV room none of this existed, only here in her parents' bedroom. She stood there for a long time, numb and confused. "That can't be true."

"That's what I thought too at first. I'm going to tell the others after supper."

"Maybe he'll change his mind."

"I don't think so."

"Where is he now?"

"I'm not sure. He came home from work in the middle of the morning, told me he wanted a divorce, then packed a suitcase and left. He said he was going to move to an apartment."

"Did he tell you who the woman was?"

"It's his secretary."

"Gloria?"

"Yes. Do you know her?"

"She typed a term paper of mine last spring, remember? Dad made me send her a thank-you card."

"I'd forgotten you knew her. Well, you'd better get started fixing supper. Ask Megan to help you."

Kimberly started to leave but then stopped. "Mom?"

"What?"

"I'm sorry."

Her mother started crying. Kimberly sat on the bed with her until Derek knocked on the door and asked when supper would be ready.

"You'd better get started," her mother said to Kimberly.

Kimberly went to the kitchen. She didn't want any help, she just wanted to be alone. Derek was making a peanut butter and jelly sandwich. She turned to face him. "Derek?"

"What?"

"Nothing."

"Why'd you call my name then?"

"Mom's going to talk to us tonight."

"It's probably about keeping the bathroom clean again. I don't know why she gets on me all the time. You and Megan are a lot worse than I'll ever be."

47

"It's not about that."

"What is it then?"

"I'll let her tell you."

"Fine, don't tell me. See if I care." He stood up to leave. "Are you crying?"

"No."

"Yes, you are. What's wrong?"

"Nothing."

"Is it about Ben?"

"No."

"What is it then?"

"I just want to be alone for a while, okay?"

He shrugged his shoulders. "Girls," he said on his way out.

Ben showed up a short time later.

"I can't work with you today. Something's come up," Kimberly said.

"What?"

"Let's go downstairs where we can talk."

They went to the office in the basement.

"Today my dad told my mom that he's in love with his secretary," she said. "He wants a divorce."

"How can he do that?"

"I don't know, but he's doing it. I know I'm not going to be much good to you for a while. I can't write love songs while my family is going through this."

"How about if I come every day for a while just to see if there's anything I can do?"

"I'd like that. Maybe you can help Megan and Derek. I'm really worried about how they're going to take this."

After supper, Megan washed the dishes while Derek, under protest, dried them. Kimberly and Ben sat at the table strangely quiet. Then Anne came out of the bedroom and announced to her children they were going to have a family council.

48

"You don't look so good," Derek said.

"I know. Ben, can you go in the living room for a few minutes? We need to meet as a family."

"I should go home now anyway," Ben said.

"No, stay," Kimberly said. "You could go down to the practice room." She paused. "Please."

"Sure, no problem."

Anne sat down at the table and gingerly touched her forehead.

"You okay?" Derek asked.

"Just a headache, that's all. Your father told me some things today that you need to know. He still loves you but he's found someone else, another woman, that he'd rather be with."

"Who?" Derek asked.

"His secretary, Gloria."

"She's too young for him," Derek said.

"Where is he now?" Megan asked.

"He moved some things out today. He won't be living here anymore."

"Where will he be staying?"

"He's getting an apartment. For the time being, if we need to get in touch with him, he said we should call him at work. He and I might be able to work things out between us. We'll just have to wait and see what happens."

"How can he be in love with someone else when he's married to you?" Derek asked. "That's not right."

"No, it isn't. He told me he and his secretary haven't done anything wrong."

"If he's in love with her, that's wrong," Megan said.

"I think what he meant is that he hasn't . . . committed adultery." She sighed. "I'm really sorry I have to talk about things like this with you kids."

"Maybe he'll change his mind and come back," Megan said.

"Maybe so."

"Doesn't he love you anymore?" Megan asked.

"I can't answer that, but one thing he wanted me to tell you all is that he still loves you."

"If he loves us, then why did he walk out?" Derek asked.

"It's not that he's unhappy with you kids. It's between him and me."

"Mom, you and Daddy will try to work things out, won't you?" Kimberly asked.

"I'm willing to try, but I'm not sure your father is. I talked to him about us going to a counselor, and he said it was too late for that. His mind seems to be made up. I don't know that there's anything we can do to change it."

"If he did change his mind, would you take him back?" Kimberly asked.

"Not with Gloria around. But with her gone, if he was willing to try and work things out, then I would too."

"There must be something we can do. We can't just sit by and watch our family be torn apart," Kimberly said.

"None of this makes any sense," Derek said.

"I know, but listen, whatever happens we're still a family. We all have to help each other. We're going to make it through this. Problems like this have always been something that happened to other people, and now it's happening to us. We just have to stick together and we'll make it. I love you kids so much. You three are the most important people in my life. And right now I need a hug." Megan was first and then Kimberly. Derek hung back until he was shamed into it by Kimberly.

"Mom, you look like you're in a lot of pain," Kimberly said when they broke up. "Why don't you go back to bed for a while? We'll be okay."

Anne stood up. "All right. My headache should go away if I just lie down and be very still and take another pill." She walked to her room and closed the door.

Derek was practicing trombone upstairs in his bedroom when Kimberly and Ben knocked on the door. He called for them to come in. They entered his room. It was so messy that the only place they could find to sit on was his unmade bed.

"Have these sheets ever been washed?" Kimberly asked.

"I don't know. Why?"

"They smell like old cheese."

"It's a new kind of detergent."

Ben looked up at the ceiling, where several pencils were stuck into the acoustic tile. "After you get the pencils stuck up there, why do you leave them?"

"It's sort of like a trophy."

"How are you doing?" Ben asked.

"Terrific, never better. Nothing fazes me. I'm sitting here playing the trombone part to 'Stars and Stripes Forever' while our family is falling apart. Nothing stops me."

"How are you feeling?" Kimberly asked.

"Hey, I don't have any feelings. That's the best way. That way nothing can hurt me."

"It's okay for a man to have feelings," Ben said.

"Maybe it's okay for some, but it's not okay for me. I don't want to talk about it to either one of you, so why don't you both just leave and let me finish practicing."

"If you ever need someone to talk to, let us know," Kimberly said.

"Yeah, yeah. Get out of here now, okay? I have work to do."

Ben and Kimberly left his room and went to Megan's door. Kimberly knocked and asked if she and Ben could come in. "Just a minute," Megan called out.

A moment later she opened the door and let them in.

Ben sat down at her desk. Her books were neatly stacked with the homework from each class ready for the next day of school. Out of curiosity, he opened her desk drawer. Pencils were stacked neatly in a tray. There was a half-empty roll of Lifesavers in the drawer, but with no extra paper and foil streaming out, the way most people handle their rolls. Her entire room showed that she had things under control.

"You want to talk about anything?" Kimberly asked.

"It's all my fault, isn't it."

"No. Why would you think that?"

She could barely say the words. "Because when we went to the Ice Capades and Daddy was late, they argued, and that started it all."

"Megan, they've been arguing for years."

"It's not only that. I'm the third child."

"What difference does that make?" Kimberly asked.

"I heard Mom tell someone once that they'd had enough money before I was born, but after I came they were always poor. You know how Mom and Dad sometimes argued over money. It must have gotten so bad that Dad couldn't stand it any longer. It's all my fault. If I'd never been born, none of this would have happened." By now tears were streaming down her face.

"It's not your fault, Megan," Kimberly said. "It's between Dad and Mom. It's not because of us."

"You can say what you want, but I know it's my fault." She continued to cry. Kimberly held her and told her again and again it wasn't her fault. When she and Ben left a few minutes later, they realized Megan still felt responsible for her parents' problems.

"Thanks for sticking around tonight," Kimberly said.

"Sure. I'd better go home now, but if anything comes up, give me a call and I'll come back," he said.

"I think we'll be okay now."

Later, as Kimberly brushed her teeth to get ready for bed, Megan came into the bathroom to talk to her. "Can I sleep in your room with you tonight?" she asked.

"Yeah, sure, if you want to."

"Is it okay if I ask Derek too?"

"Why?"

"So we can all be together. He can sleep on the floor in his sleeping bag."

"I guess so."

Megan went to Derek's room. "I'm sleeping in Kimberly's room," she said. "Want to be with us?"

"Not really."

"We'll all be together. It's like when we went camping at Yellowstone. You could sleep next to the bed on the floor in your sleeping bag."

"It's a dumb idea."

"But you'll go along with it because I asked you, right?" Megan said.

"All right."

Derek grabbed his sleeping bag and followed Megan into Kimberly's room. He lay down on the floor next to the bed.

"Derek, you have to clear out of here in the morning when we need to get dressed," Kimberly warned.

"I know that," Derek said.

"Now everybody go to sleep, okay?" Kimberly said.

"If someone has to use the bathroom during the night," Derek said, "be sure and watch where you're walking, because I'm down here."

"What's the matter, Derek?" Kimberly said. "Don't you want a footprint on your face in the morning?"

Megan, in the bed, was just a few inches above Derek on the floor. "Kimberly is fun, isn't she?" she said softly to Derek.

"Yeah."

"You think Dad will miss her?"

"Yeah."

"Enough to make him come back?"

"Probably."

"That's what I think too," Megan said just before she fell asleep.

6

Sunday began cold and cloudy and got worse as the day progressed. It started snowing just before the family left for church. It was the first time they had gone to church as a family without a father.

As they walked into the chapel for the beginning of Sunday School, a counselor in the elders quorum presidency came up and asked Anne where her husband was.

"He won't be here today," she said.

"I wanted to ask him how he's doing on his home teaching. Do you know if he's gone this month yet?"

"No, I don't know."

"I need the report today."

"I can't help you."

"Could you have him call me?"

"I'll give him your message."

"Thanks." He glanced down at a sheet of paper and set off to find someone else.

"Doesn't anybody know about Dad yet?" Kimberly asked her mother.

"Not yet. I have a meeting with the bishop this afternoon."

"Why haven't you told anybody?" Kimberly asked.

"I thought your father might come back."

Later, as they sat together in the chapel before sacrament

meeting started, Derek leaned forward to rest his head on the pew in front of them. Kimberly started touching him on the back. "What are you doing?" he complained.

"Picking lint balls off your sweater."

"Don't. I like 'em there."

"Let's play 'Guess What I'm Writing.' "

It was a game they'd played since they were kids. She would write on his back with her finger and he'd try to guess what she'd written.

She traced out several letters on his back. "Well?" she said.

"I'm too old for this."

"I'll try it again. This time concentrate."

When she was through, he was clueless.

"Give up?"

"Yes."

"It was, 'Get your Eagle.' "

He sat back in the pew so she'd have nothing to write on.

"When are you going to get your Eagle?" she asked.

"Never. That was Dad's idea, and now he's gone."

"You're so close to getting it. You can't quit now."

"Why don't you go pick lint balls off Megan?"

"She doesn't have any."

The bishop stood up and welcomed everyone to sacrament meeting. Kimberly quit talking but did write the word *Eagle* with her finger on Derek's arm.

After church was over, Gina, a sophomore like Derek, came over to talk to him.

"Are you going to the dance after the game at school next Friday?" she asked.

"I don't know."

"If you go, maybe I'll see you there."

"Yeah, maybe," he said with little enthusiasm. It wasn't that he disliked Gina. It was just that, for him then, she seemed a little too sincere. She answered questions in class and stood up and cheered for the school team at pep assemblies. She was elected secretary for student senate in school because everyone knew there wasn't anybody who could take better minutes than Gina. All of this Derek held against her.

"Sometimes people go out for pizza after a dance. What do you think about that?"

He wasn't sure if she was asking him to go with her for pizza after the dance or if she just wanted his opinion about people who eat pizza after a dance. "It's all right, I guess."

"I have money, but we'd need to catch a ride from someone," she said.

He shrugged his shoulders. "Whatever."

After church the family went home and had soup and sandwiches, and then Anne left to go see the bishop to tell him about her husband.

"I'm going upstairs to take a nap," Kimberly said. "Ben's coming over in a while. Wake me up when he comes. And don't mess up the house. Okay?"

After Kimberly left, Derek started wondering where Gloria lived. He went to the kitchen and got the phone book and brought it back to his room, then knocked on Kimberly's door. She mumbled something, so he opened her door. "What's Gloria's last name?"

"Montgomery," she said sleepily. "What are you going to do?"

"Nothing."

"Whatever you're thinking of doing, don't do it."

"I'm not going to do anything. Go back to sleep."

He looked up Gloria's address in the phone book. She lived in an apartment building less than a mile from their home. He memorized her phone number, then went to the phone in the kitchen and punched in her number. When she answered, he hung up. *Let her worry about that for a while,* he thought.

He wanted to know if his father was at her apartment. He looked outside. It was snowing hard, but that didn't bother him. He put on his jacket and gloves. Just as he was about to leave, he saw Ben walking up the sidewalk. He opened the door for him. "Kimberly's taking a nap. Ask Megan to go and wake her up," he said.

"Where are you going?" Ben asked.

"For a walk."

"It's not very good weather for a walk."

"I don't care, I'm still going."

"Do you want me to take you somewhere?"

"No. It's only a few blocks."

"To where?"

"I want to find out if my dad's at Gloria's apartment."

"I need some exercise. Is it okay if I walk with you?"

Derek shrugged. "Whatever."

Walking in the snow made it hard for him to stay mad, especially with Ben along. They had a contest to see who could hit the most stop signs with snowballs.

He was almost feeling good until they came to the apartment building where Gloria lived and he saw his father's car in the parking lot. He wrote "I hate you" in the snow on the hood of the car. Ben stood by and watched.

"Why didn't you try and stop me?" Derek said as they headed toward the entrance of the apartment building.

"You weren't doing any harm."

"I hate him, you know."

They went inside the building, looked at the names on the mailboxes, and found that Gloria lived on the third floor in apartment 317. They took the stairs.

"What are you going to do?" Ben asked.

"I haven't decided yet."

"Don't do anything stupid that'll get you in trouble."

"I don't care anymore."

"If you get in trouble, then I get in trouble too, because I'm with you."

"Leave me then."

"No."

"Why not?"

"Because we're friends."

"We are? That's news to me. Just because you're a friend of Kimberly's doesn't mean you're my friend."

"I'd like to be your friend."

When they got to apartment 317, Derek stopped and put his ear to the door for a while, then continued down the hall.

"What did you hear?"

"The football game on TV. My dad is watching TV on a Sunday. That figures. We could never even watch the Super Bowl, even when it was after church. He's such a hypocrite. From now on I don't have to live by any of the rules he ever gave me. I've been missing out on life all these years. I guess it's time I changed all that. I don't know where to start. Maybe I'll get drunk this weekend, or maybe I'll get in a fight at school, or maybe I'll start smoking. There's so many things to choose from, I don't know where to start. I can do anything I want from now on. But no matter what I do, it won't be half as bad as what my father has done to us." Suddenly he ran down the stairs and out the building. Ben ran after him.

Derek ran to his father's car. The snow that had fallen since they'd gone inside was beginning to cover up his message. He started kicking the tires of the car with his foot and hit the side of the car with his fist, but all it did was hurt his hand, so he looked around for a large rock to throw at his dad's precious car, but everything was covered up with snow.

"C'mon, Derek, we need to go home."

"How can he get away with this? Why doesn't anybody send him to his room? Or take away his privileges? How can he just walk away from us and have nobody stop him? I wish I had a stick of dynamite so I could blow up his stupid car into a million pieces!"

A car pulled into the parking lot.

"Derek, we need to go now."

"No, not until I've paid him back for what he's doing to our family."

The driver of the other car got out and saw them standing there. "You two live here?" he asked.

"No," Ben said.

"Then you don't have any business here. Get out of here or I'm calling the police."

"I don't have to do what you say," Derek shot back. He hit the window of his dad's car with his fist.

"Hey, stop that!" the man shouted.

"Come and make me, you jerk face!"

The man came after Derek but slipped on the ice and fell down.

"What's the matter, can't you even stand up?" Derek shouted.

The man swore at Derek and came after him.

Derek turned and ran away. Ben ran after him. The two of them cut down an alley and then through somebody's yard. They zigzagged from one block to another until they were sure the man was no longer following them. Then they slowed down and walked in the snow.

"I know why God invented snow," Derek said.

"Why?"

"Because he knew how rotten things were going to get and sometimes he can't stand it either, so he just covers everything up, all the garbage cans, all the junked-out cars, all the families that are falling apart, all the husbands in their secretaries' apartments while their wives are bawling their eyes out. I think sometimes God just covers everything up with snow and lets it be nice and white and clean for a little while. That's what I'd do if I were God."

"I think you're probably right."

When they got home, Anne was still gone. The first thing Derek did was turn on the TV as loud as he could. Ben asked Megan to tell Kimberly he was there.

Then Anne came home. "Why is the TV on?" she asked.

"It doesn't matter anymore," Derek said. "Those were Dad's rules, and he's gone."

"They're the rules of our family. Turn it off."

"Not until my program is over."

She walked over and turned the TV off.

"That's not fair," he complained.

"What makes you think it isn't fair?"

"Dad was the one who set up the rule, and now he's at Gloria's apartment watching football on TV."

"How do you know that?"

"Ben and I went there and walked by his apartment and stopped and listened."

"Did you go in?"

"No."

"You must never go there unless you're invited."

"Is he living with her?" Derek asked.

"No, he has an apartment."

"That's what he says, but how can we believe anything he says anymore? Do you hate him now?"

"No. I'm just very disappointed in him."

"Well, you can be disappointed if you want; but as for me, I hate him."

"He's still your father."

"Then why isn't he acting like a father?"

"I don't know. I'm sorry you children have to be subjected to this. The bishop is going to try to talk to him and let him know how serious what he's doing is."

"That's all? He falls in love with his secretary and all that happens is the bishop talks to him? That doesn't sound very bad to me. I got a C in math and had all my privileges taken away. He walks away from his family, and all that happens to him is the bishop talks to him."

"If he doesn't change his ways, he may end up losing his

membership in the church and his family and the trust of his children and his marriage."

"I bet he doesn't care about any of that. Gloria must be worth more to him than any of us. In a way I don't blame him."

"What do you mean?"

"All he got from us was problems. Megan has to have braces, Kimberly needs money for college, and you need him to do jobs around the house."

"What do you need?" his mother asked.

"I don't need anything from him or anybody. I don't feel anything, I don't need anything. I just want people to leave me alone." He bounded up the stairs to his room and slammed the door.

Anne focused her attention on Ben. "You went with Derek to Gloria's place?"

"Yes. I wasn't sure what he had in mind so I thought I'd better go along just in case."

Anne nodded. "I appreciate you looking out for my son."

"Sure, no problem."

Wednesday morning when they went out to go to school, the car wouldn't start. Anne tried it several times, but all it did was make a clicking noise.

"I have to be on campus by eight o'clock," Kimberly said.

"I'm doing the best I can," Anne snapped.

"You don't have to bite my head off."

"Sorry, this is just so frustrating, not knowing anything about cars. Your father has always taken care of things like this."

The car still wouldn't start. Finally Anne called a neighbor for rides for Derek and Megan, and Kimberly phoned Ben and asked him for a ride.

Before Derek and Megan left to go next door, Derek asked his mother what she was going to do about the car.

"If I call your father, I know he'll come and get it started."

"Don't call him."

"Why not?"

"We don't need him anymore."

"If I call a service station, they'll charge me a fortune."

"It's worth it not to have to see Dad again. I don't ever want to see him again."

She looked at him for a long time without saying anything. "Derek, I know this is hard for you. With all my heart, I wish you didn't have to go through this."

"I'll learn all about cars, and then I'll be able to help out like Dad did."

"I know you will, Derek. You're a good boy. I know I can depend on you to help out."

Every day in study hour Megan took a few minutes to write in her diary. This is what she wrote that day:

Why can't I have a perfect life? I mean my dad is in love with his secretary and probably is going to get a divorce. I feel so sorry for my mom because she is all alone now and she has to try to keep the family together all by herself. I can't imagine walking into school and saying that my dad and mom might get a divorce.

I wish I was more like Kimberly. She's so lucky. She's almost through being a teenager.

That evening at supper, Anne asked Derek if he was going to scouts that night. He said he wasn't. She asked why not. He said he didn't feel like it.

"You'd better finish up so you can get your Eagle."

"I don't care about that anymore."

"You put all that work into it, and you're so close to getting it now. It would be a shame not to get it."

"The only reason I worked on it was because Dad wanted me to, and he's not here anymore."

62

"I want you to get it," Anne said.

"Don't I have any say in this?"

Kimberly stepped in. "Derek, quit being such a jerk. We all want you to get your Eagle. Do it for the family."

"What family? We don't have a family anymore."

He didn't go to scouts but instead stayed in his room and tried to do homework. Gina phoned him. He talked to her mainly because he felt sorry for her. He decided she must not have many friends to keep calling him all the time when all he did was go "uh-huh" to whatever she said. He realized that he might be the only guy at school who said anything to her. She told him how much she was looking forward to the dance on Friday night at school. He wondered if he'd spend his entire life talking to people nobody else wanted to talk to.

After supper Ben came over to see if he could fix their car. Kimberly went out with him and stood in the cold and held the flashlight for him.

"When a car doesn't start, most of the time it's because of corroded battery terminals," he said. After he finished cleaning the terminals, he tried to start the car. This time it worked.

"Yes! Mr. Hardware to the rescue!" Kimberly cheered, kissing him on the cheek.

He smiled. "I guess I've learned a few things from my dad."

"I should do something to show my appreciation. How about if we work on a new song?"

"Sure, that's always fun."

"But not here. Can we go to your apartment?"

"I'd better call and ask my aunt if it'd be okay. She's still recovering from the last time I had Julia over."

"Tell her I'm not going with anybody who's crazy, deranged, or an escaped convict."

Ben laughed. "She'll be so pleased to hear that."

Fifteen minutes later Ben and Kimberly were on their way.

"What's your aunt like?" she asked.

"Her first name is Elizabeth. She works for the Church.

She has more white blouses than just about anyone I've ever met. She likes music, but her tastes run more toward classical music. We go to concerts together. I think she's trying to give me some culture. She told me that next week she's going to come to Angelo's and hear us sing."

They stopped off at a store to get some grape juice and crackers and then continued on their way to his aunt's place.

When they walked in the house, he made the introductions. "Kimberly, it's so nice to meet you," his aunt said. Then she turned to Ben. "She's a lovely girl, Ben. You can bring her here anytime you want."

Ben led Kimberly up the narrow stairs to his apartment. "One of the rules about having a girl here is that I keep the door to the stairs open. My aunt is very protective of me."

"Good for her."

His apartment was in what was formerly the attic. Two of the walls were slanted to match the roof line. At one end of the small living room was a tiny area for a kitchen. A door at the other end of the living room led to his bedroom. He wouldn't let her go into that room, explaining that he hadn't made the bed that day.

The living room had a couch, a table to eat and study on, an oval throw rug in the middle of the floor, a CD player, Ben's guitar, and some posters of seagulls his aunt had put on the wall before he moved in. He told Kimberly that he didn't much care for the pictures but didn't have the heart to take them down. The best part of the room was a gable that extended out from the window. A built-in platform filled with fluffy pillows allowed a person to sit in the gable and look out at the lights of the city.

He poured them both a glass of grape juice and dumped the crackers into a bowl. Then they sat with crossed legs on the ledge in the gable and sipped their grape juice and munched on the crackers.

"Let's not work on a new song," he said. "Let's just talk."

"Okay."

"I know you're going through a hard time, and I want to be here for you when you need someone."

"Thanks."

"What do you need from me now?"

She handed him her empty glass. "Some more grape juice."

He jumped up and got the pitcher from the refrigerator and filled her glass. "What else do you need?"

"Ben, what do you want me to do? Pour out my soul to you?"

"Okay, what do *you* want to do?" he asked.

"I want to sit here and look out at the lights of the city and listen to some music. Don't ask me how I'm feeling. Don't tell me that other families go through divorces and get through it just fine. Just don't try so hard."

They sat and listened to music and looked out at the city lights and drank grape juice.

After a while she said, "I feel better now."

"I'm glad. I wish I could help you."

"I know you do. You know what? It's a lot harder than I thought it would be. I've had friends who had parents go through a divorce. For the most part I didn't do much to even show I cared about what was happening. And now it's happening to me. Sometimes I wonder why people aren't trying to help us out more, but then I think about what I did when my friends went through it."

He stood up. "Tonight I'm going to take you away from all your troubles."

"How are you going to manage that?"

He took her hand and led her to a throw rug in the entrance to his room. "Sit down. This is a magic carpet. It can take you wherever you want to go, anywhere in time, anywhere in space," he said. He turned off the lights then lit a candle. They sat on his throw rug facing each other.

His aunt called up. "Ben, did the power go out up there?"

65

"It's okay. We're just talking."

"All right. I'm baking some cookies. I'll bring them up in a few minutes."

"Thanks."

Kimberly smiled. "Everyone should have an aunt like yours."

"I agree. Decide where you want to go on your magic carpet tonight. Just close your eyes and make a wish."

She closed her eyes and said, smiling, "I wish I wasn't with such a goofball tonight."

He tiptoed into the bathroom and closed the door.

She opened her eyes. "It's a miracle!"

When Ben came out, he had a ridiculous-looking green towel with pink floral print wrapped around his head. Kimberly, seeing him, laughed until her sides ached.

"Good evening," he said in a fake accent. "My name is Shammim. I'll be your genie this evening. Make a wish, my lady, and I will take you wherever you wish to be taken."

On another day it might have worked and she would have let Ben take her to a land of make-believe. But there was too much pain and uncertainty in her life now for that.

She sighed. "Take me back to the way it was in our family before my dad met Gloria."

The magic was gone. His shoulders slumped. "I wish I could do that."

"Me too. You want to know what I really would like to do tonight? I want to go talk to my dad. Will you take me there?"

"This is the address my dad gave. It's where he's having his mail forwarded to. But he might not be here," Kimberly said as they climbed the stairs in the apartment building. "He's probably over at Gloria's."

They knocked on the door. After a minute her father opened it. "Kimberly, I didn't expect you."

"You remember Ben, don't you?"

"Yes, of course. What can I do for you?"

"I need to talk to you. Is that all right?"

"Yes, of course. Come on in. I was just catching up on some paperwork." He picked up some papers, stuffed them in his briefcase, and turned off the small black and white TV. "Sit down."

Kimberly and Ben sat on a well-worn couch. Her father sat on a kitchen chair.

There was a long, awkward silence. "I'm sorry for what I'm putting the family through," her father finally said. "I know it hasn't been easy on you kids. I still care about you and Derek and Megan."

"If you really cared about us, you wouldn't have fallen in love with Gloria and you wouldn't have left us."

"Someday you'll understand how it was with me."

"I don't think I'll ever understand that."

"As you get older, it gets harder to decide what to do in certain situations."

"It's not hard for a lot of adults to live the right way. Why is it so hard for you?"

"In the beginning I didn't know this was going to happen. Gloria and I haven't done anything wrong."

"Have you ever kissed her?"

His father looked at her strangely. "Why would you ask a question like that?"

"You have kissed her, haven't you? When you kissed her, was it during the time you were supposed to be at work? And if it was, when you came home that day after work, did you act like nothing happened? Did you walk in and kiss Mom the way you usually did? Do you remember what you said to me that night?"

"This is not appropriate for us to discuss."

"I think it is. I just keep wondering if it was one of the nights you encouraged Derek to finish his Eagle project or if it was one of the nights you told me to be careful what kind

67

of guys I spent time with. Or was it one of those nights you told us we were going to be a forever family and that we'd be together even in heaven? Do you remember what you said to us the night you kissed Gloria for the first time?"

"You don't know any of the circumstances surrounding this."

"Maybe I don't, but I also don't understand how you could tell Gloria you loved her and then come home and act like nothing was wrong."

He didn't answer for a long time, and then he said, "I never meant to hurt your mother."

"Well, in case you don't know it, you *have* hurt her."

"I know that, and I'm sorry."

"Sorry enough to come back to us?"

"I can't do that."

"Why not? Because you love Gloria? Well, you loved Mom too once, didn't you? So what's the difference? There's only one of Gloria, so you'll hurt fewer people if you leave her. Besides, you might leave Gloria in a year or two."

"I'm sure that won't happen."

"How can you be so sure of what you will or won't do? If you ask me, you don't seem to have much self-control. I have a lot more of that than you do. At least I'm still living the way you told me to live. And you're not."

"Someday you'll understand this better."

"What is it that I need to understand?"

He sighed. "Okay, I guess you deserve to know the truth. I haven't wanted to tell you, but your mother and I had grown apart over the last few years. Somehow the spark was gone. We were just going through the motions of being happily married. Gloria isn't the villain in all of this."

"Okay, but if things weren't right in your marriage, why didn't you do anything to make it better? Why didn't you go to a counselor? Why just abandon everything and go chasing after Gloria? Don't even try to make me understand this. The way I see it, either a person lives the right way or he doesn't. And now I know you don't. I won't ever understand it because it's wrong what you're doing, and nothing you can ever say is going to change that. What was so awful with Mom anyway? Wasn't she thin enough for you? You could have told her to lose some weight and she would've done it. She would have done anything you asked her. She'd have even dyed her hair to get rid of some of the gray, if that's what you wanted. She would have done anything for you if you'd asked her, but you had to turn to someone else. It's not right and you know it, so don't ever lecture me again about what I do, because whatever I do from now on will never be as awful as what you've done."

Her father glanced at Ben. "I don't think Ben should be listening to this."

"Why not? I tell him everything. Actually, I tell everyone who will listen. I want everyone to know what it's like to have a hypocrite as a father."

"Kimberly, you may not believe this, but the thing that's been the hardest on me is knowing how much this was going to hurt you and Derek and Megan. I am truly sorry for the pain I've caused you kids."

"What about Derek? You were his hero, and now he doesn't have any heroes. I think that's pretty rotten for a boy not to have any heroes."

He sighed. "I am sorry . . . but nothing you can say is going to change the way things are."

"Maybe not, but I had to say it anyway." She stood up. "I've lost all the respect I ever had for you. Good-bye."

She and Ben got back in his car.

"Thank you for going with me." She sounded emotionally drained.

"Yeah, sure."

"Do you think I was too hard on him?"

"No."

"Boy, I could really use that magic carpet of yours now. Let's escape to a tropical island, whattaya say?"

"Do you want to go back to my apartment now?"

"I want to go somewhere and forget everything that's happening in my family. Everything is so messed up." She wiped her eyes. "I guess you'd better take me home. I still have some studying to do."

"Okay." He paused. "Have you met Gloria?"

"Yes. Last year when she typed a paper for me."

"What's she like?"

"She's looks a little like Demi Moore—short hair, a great face, a kind of whispery voice, nice smile. She's okay but she's not that great. I mean, she's not the kind of a woman I'd pick as one that a man would abandon his wife and family for." She looked out the window, then turned back to face him. "I don't think she tried to break up my dad's marriage. She's just not the type. That's just it. I don't know what made my dad do what he did. If it can happen to my dad, maybe it can happen to any man. Maybe you'll do the same thing someday to your wife. I mean, how can anyone predict what's going to happen? When my mom was my age, how could she have known that she shouldn't marry my dad because of what he would do to her someday? How can anyone know for sure who they can trust?"

"I don't have the answer to that," he said.

"I don't think anyone does. Sometimes I'm not so sure I even want to get married."

"Everyone feels that way once in a while."

"Do you?"

"Yes, sometimes," he said.

"Why?"

"Being married is a big responsibility."

"Hey, just living is a big responsibility."

He took her home and then went to his apartment and sat overlooking the city and played their songs. He could still smell traces of her perfume in the alcove where she had been sitting.

7

Friday night Derek went to the basketball game at school. He didn't intend to stay for the dance afterwards, but then some friends talked him into it. The instant he walked out on the floor, Gina was waiting for him like a vulture. She was all smiles, but it didn't do any good because he felt mean.

The two of them stood around and watched people dance. She asked if he wanted to dance and he said no. She asked what he wanted to do. He was about to say "Nothing with you," but then he looked at her, so hopeful, smelling of shampoo and perfume. He knew how much work Kimberly went through when she got ready for a date. He knew Gina had done the same thing, and so all of a sudden he felt sorry for her because he didn't think anyone else would ask her to dance. It wasn't that there was anything really wrong with her—she just tried too hard.

"Gina, you look . . . uh . . . okay tonight."

She smiled like it was the most wonderful thing anybody had ever said to her. He knew he was trapped for the rest of the night. He asked if she wanted to dance. Her smile got bigger, and she said yes.

As they danced, he could tell this was a big deal to her, even though he felt like he was a million miles away. He wondered why she went to all this trouble for a stupid dance.

After they danced for a while, he left her and went out to

71

the hall and found some guys to talk with. It was a lot more fun there, but then they had a girls' choice and Gina found him, so he had to dance with her again. She asked if he was going with Jason and MacKenzie to Pizza Hut after the dance.

"I dunno. Maybe."

After the dance he went with her in Jason's car to Pizza Hut. She turned to him and smiled. That's when he realized she didn't know what he was thinking. He thought that maybe nobody ever knows what anyone else is thinking. Maybe it's the same with adults. He thought, *Maybe Mom thought Dad loved her and would never leave her, but maybe Dad didn't think that at all. Maybe Dad never did love her. Maybe he was just pushed into everything because Mom smiled at him all the time the way Gina smiles at me in that kind of a happy, trusting smile.* He looked out the car window and felt more depressed than ever before in his life.

At Pizza Hut, after they got seated and ordered, Jason wanted to show off how good he was at video games, so everyone crowded around to watch him play. He was good, so the game kept going for a long time. After a while MacKenzie, Gina, and Derek got bored watching and returned to their table.

Gina excused herself to go to the restroom, which left MacKenzie and Derek alone together at the booth. MacKenzie had long blonde hair that cascaded down in bold and brassy curls. She had a great smile, which she was flashing a lot more since she got her braces off. She loved life and being with boys and wasn't afraid to show it.

For a few minutes Derek had more fun with her than with any other girl he'd ever been with. They started talking about what would happen if the pizza came while Jason and Gina were gone and he and MacKenzie ate it all. What would they say when they were asked about it? They each came up with ideas, and most of them were dumb, but they were both in a crazy mood, and they started laughing. Derek loved to make her laugh. He found himself wishing this could go on for the rest of his life. Not only that, but he felt like she must be feeling the same way, so he asked her if she'd go with him, but she said she was going with Jason.

"I know that, but you could always break up with him, couldn't you?"

"Yes, I guess so."

"Then why don't you do it?"

"What about Gina?"

"I don't care about her."

"Why are you going with her then?"

"I'm not. Tonight was her idea. I'd rather go with you."

He reached out and held her hand under the table. She didn't try to pull away from him. He took his fingertips and ran them down the palm of her hand. She closed her eyes, and he knew she liked it a lot.

Jason, still playing the video game, glanced in their direction and called out, "I'm already on Level Nine."

They smiled at each other. "Great, Jason," Derek said, all the while holding MacKenzie's hand under the table. "We are too," he said, softly enough so that only MacKenzie could hear it.

"Stop," she giggled.

"Let's go lock Gina in the restroom."

"You wouldn't want to do that."

"Yes, I would. You're more fun. You like me, don't you?"

"Yes."

"I like you too. I've always liked you. This is fun. Jason doesn't suspect a thing, does he?"

"No. When he's playing a video game, he doesn't think about anything else," she said.

When Gina came back, Derek felt a little guilty because she had only been gone five minutes and he'd already asked another girl to go with him. Because he knew how it was with Kimberly and Megan, he knew that all the time Gina was in the restroom she was probably doing things so that she'd look better for him, and while she was doing that, he was flirting with another girl. He wondered if his mother was like Gina when she was a girl. Gina smiled at him, and that made him feel even worse.

When the pizza was served, Jason quit playing his video game and came back to the booth. "It's too bad you're no good at games, Derek. We could have played partners."

"What am I good at?" Derek asked.

"Nothing that I can think of," Jason teased.

"I can think of something," Derek said, glancing at MacKenzie, who blushed.

After MacKenzie finished eating, she dropped her arm that was closest to him and rested her hand on the seat. Derek dropped his hand too and held hers. She started blushing but didn't move away.

Suddenly Gina cried out, "What are you doing?" One look at her and he knew she'd seen him holding MacKenzie's hand. MacKenzie pulled away.

"I need to go home now," Gina said, standing up quickly. "I'm going to call my mom to come pick me up." She grabbed her coat and started to put it on.

"What's wrong?" Jason asked.

"Derek was fooling around with MacKenzie under the table," she said.

Jason glared at Derek, who protested, "We were just holding hands. It didn't mean anything. The whole thing was just a joke. You don't have to make such a big deal out of it. The only reason I did it was because I was bored." It was the truth, but it was the wrong thing for Gina to hear. She stared at him. "Gina, I didn't mean it that way," he said quickly. "Look, I'm sorry I messed up. I guess I'd better go now."

He walked home. Along the way, he passed a pay phone. He dialed Gloria's number and hung up when she answered it. At home he lay in bed and wondered if he would have any friends on Sunday at church or on Monday at school. He felt worse than he had ever felt before in his life. He wanted to talk to someone, but there was nobody who would understand how he felt. He went to his room and paced the floor. Then he went downstairs and turned on the TV.

Because she had two exams the next Monday, Kimberly had asked Ben to take her home after they played at Angelo's that Friday night. She studied until midnight and then went to bed. But she couldn't sleep, so she went downstairs and saw that Derek was still up. She sat down with him. He told her what had happened after the dance. She suggested that he call and apologize to Gina the next day. He said he didn't want to. She said she'd help him. He reluctantly agreed to try it and then went to bed.

She watched TV for a while and then went to bed, but she still couldn't sleep. Finally, at one-thirty she called Ben. He answered on the first ring.

"Were you asleep?" she asked.

"No. I was just going over some of our songs."

"I can't sleep."

"Me either. You want to drive around for a while?"

"Sure."

He picked her up ten minutes later. "Where do you want to go?" he asked.

"I don't care."

"Did you get any studying done?"

"Some. I still have a little left for tomorrow. What did you get done?"

"I just had a reading assignment for the weekend. I got that done and then went through all our songs."

"What for?" she asked.

"Just something to do." He paused. "Every song reminds me of you. By the time I was done, I was really missing you, so I'm glad you called."

75

"Right now being with you and away from my family is the only good part of my life," she said. "You don't know what it's like for me at home. Sometimes I just want to run away from it all, to have even just a little bit of time when I feel comforted and safe and secure. The only time I feel that way is when I'm with you. Everything is pressing down on me. Suddenly it's like I'm responsible for Derek and Megan, and they're both falling apart a little at a time. I try to help, but it doesn't do any good. Tonight Derek got in trouble with his friends after a dance. And Megan's starting to clam up. I don't know what she's thinking half the time. And my classes are so hard. All my teachers are having a race to see how fast they can cover the material.

"I'm not supposed to have all this dumped on me. I'm not the mother—I'm just one of the kids. On top of that, I don't know how I'm going to pay for books and tuition next quarter. I don't know if my dad will pay for any of it from now on. I've never been more uncertain about my future. Sometimes I get so depressed, I just want to forget all my troubles. See, the thing is, I have to be strong for Megan, and I have to be strong for Derek, and my Mom is doing all she can, so I don't want to bring her down with my problems. Sometimes it gets to be too much for me. Like tonight. You're the only one I can talk to, the only one I can open up to, the only one I can be totally honest with."

"I want to help you any way I can."

"I know you do, and that means a lot to me."

No sooner had they pulled into the driveway an hour later than her mother marched out to the car.

"Oh no, we're in trouble now," Kimberly said, rolling down the window to talk to her mother.

"What is going on here?" Anne asked. "You just walk out of the house in the middle of the night without telling me where you're going?"

"I couldn't sleep."

"Where did you go?"

"We just drove around."

"At this time of night? Good grief, Kimberly, don't I have enough to worry about? I want you inside the house right now." Her mother headed back to the house.

"I'll talk to her so she won't think this was your fault," Kimberly said, kissing him on the cheek. Then she got out of the car and hurried inside.

The next day, Saturday, was as bleak a day as any that had come before it. When Anne came home from looking for a job, she found a carton of milk that had been left out since morning. With money as tight as it was, she called her family together and, with tears in her eyes, lectured them on how much a carton of milk cost.

During supper there were still all kinds of undercurrents of anger and bad feelings. Anne was still upset about Kimberly sneaking out of the house the night before to be with Ben. Kimberly felt that her mother didn't give her credit for taking on many of the responsibilities in the family. Derek was angry with the world because of rumors and gossip going around about him and MacKenzie at Pizza Hut the night before. And Megan could hardly stand the tension brought on by everyone else. She wished she had the courage to tell her mother she wished she could move in with some other family.

Into this hostile environment came, unannounced, visitors. The doorbell rang.

"If that's Ben, tell him you can't go out tonight," Anne said firmly to Kimberly.

"Mother, I'm in college now. Don't you think I'm a little too old for you to ground me?"

"If you live here, you go by the same rules as everyone else."

"Isn't someone going to answer the door?" Megan complained.

77

"You've got legs, Megan. Answer it yourself," Kimberly snapped.

Megan went to the door. In the kitchen the rest of the family could hear a man with a booming voice. "Hi there, is your mother home?"

Anne, thinking that if it was a salesman she would make short work of him, got up from the table and marched to the door.

It was Robert Hatch, a member of their ward, and Mike Jefferson, a deacon. Brother Hatch was retired. He and his wife had just returned home from a mission. "Sorry, we tried to call, but I kept getting a busy signal. The bishop asked me and Mike here to be your new home teachers. We were in the neighborhood and thought we'd drop by some banana bread. My wife made some today, but she forgot and doubled the recipe like she used to when our kids were around, so Mike and I are going around trying to get people to take it from us before it gets old and stale. It's just out of the oven."

Derek heard the magic words and came out of the kitchen to get the banana bread. It smelled wonderful. He took it into the kitchen, and a minute later, he and Megan went back to the living room, each with a slice of banana bread in their hands. "This is great stuff," Derek said, talking with his mouth full.

"It sure is," Megan agreed.

"Well, good, I'll tell my wife you like it. Look, we can't stay long. I just wanted you to know we'll be coming around, probably more often than you want us, but, you know, I don't have much else to do with my time. Whenever I go home, my wife keeps trying to put me to work." He had a rich, contagious laugh. "You know how that goes."

"Please sit down, won't you?" Anne asked.

Brother Hatch and Mike sat down. Brother Hatch's hair had turned white long ago but it didn't matter—he was still a handsome man. Mike was glad to be going home teaching with a man who treated him to ice cream after every visit.

"Well," Brother Hatch said, "I understand from what the bishop told me that things maybe aren't going the way you'd like in your family. Is that right?" He focused his gaze on Anne, and then on Kimberly, and then on Derek and Megan. He seemed to be looking for clues to how each of them was doing. "I don't have answers for most of what happens in this world," he said. "People do get hurt, innocent people, people who have done nothing to deserve the way life is treating them. I don't know why that is, but I've seen it enough to know that life is not always fair."

He looked again at each of them in turn and then said, "I've had a few disappointments in my life too, things that I couldn't understand why they were happening to me. Some I never did find out why they happened. There is something I have found, though, that I can always count on, and that is prayer. When you feel the worst, you can always go to Heavenly Father and ask him to help you get through the hard times. I've been disappointed by a lot of people, people I thought I could trust, but I've never been disappointed by God." He paused. "Excuse me for asking, but are you folks having family prayer?"

"Most of the time," Anne said.

"Good for you. And what about personal prayer? Kimberly?"

Everyone looked at Kimberly. "Not very much lately," she said slowly.

"What about that, Kimberly? Here you are, going through one of the hardest experiences a son or a daughter can go through, and you're not asking for help from the one person who loves you and can help you more than anyone else."

"Can he bring our dad back home?" she asked.

"He doesn't force people to do what they don't want to do."

"Then how will it help to pray?" Derek asked.

"I don't know for sure, Derek. Why don't you try it and then tell me?"

Next he turned to Megan. "Megan, how are you handling this?"

"There's no problem with Megan," Derek said quickly.

"Somtimes those are the ones you need to worry about the most. Why don't we let Megan tell us how Megan is doing."

"I'm doing okay," Megan said, but with no eye contact.

"Derek, what about you? How are you taking all this?"

"I don't feel a thing."

Brother Hatch reached over and rested his hand on Derek's knee. "Let's talk about that sometime, okay?"

"I don't need to talk about anything."

"Maybe you will sometime though. If you do, I'm always home, getting in my wife's way. Come over anytime."

Derek just shrugged his shoulders.

"Sister Madison, how are things going with you?"

"I'm not sure. Sometimes I'm not a very good mother to my kids. I want to be, but sometimes — well, like today, I jumped all over them because someone left the milk out." Tears began streaming down her face. "Sometimes I'm not sure if they even know how much I love them. I don't say it enough, not like I used to."

"Why don't you say it now?" Brother Hatch said.

She looked at him a moment, then turned toward her family and said, "Kids, I love you a million times more than some silly carton of spoiled milk."

By then everyone was having to deal with tears. Brother Hatch turned to his companion and said, "Well, Mike, we've stayed too long already. Sister Madison, could we have a word of prayer before we leave?"

Anne asked Mike to say the prayer.

"Why are you our home teachers now?" Anne asked as she walked with them to the door.

"Because the bishop asked us," he said. "If he had more time, he'd come here himself to be your home teacher, but he's a pretty busy man, so he sent us. I have a little more time to devote to things like this than a man who has to make a living. I'm all done with that."

"Thank you for coming."

"I meant what I said. Call me anytime you need someone. If Mike's not available, I'll bring my wife. She's better at things like this than I am anyway." He stood up and clasped Anne's hands in his. "You know, our daughter got a divorce a few years ago and she's had to go it alone, so I know a little bit about what you're going through. I know it's not easy to raise a family all by yourself. If you need help, you let us know. I mean it. Here's my phone number. Call me anytime, day or night."

She thanked them for coming, said goodbye at the door, and watched them walk away.

The visit hadn't solved any of her problems, but she was glad Brother Hatch was her home teacher.

8

Megan walked in the door after school on Monday. Compared to Kimberly and Derek, she had always been the one who made the least noise when she entered the house. This time was no exception. Her mother, who was on the phone with her father, didn't hear her come in.

"I don't know why you're saying it's unreasonable," she heard her mother say. "I think it's very reasonable. All I'm asking for is that I get to keep the house and a little child support . . . They're your children too, Paul. What do you want to do, send them out on the street to fend for themselves? . . . You can't be serious. That won't cover even food and the house payment . . . I'll get a lawyer, Paul, you can be sure about that . . . Sell the house? Why should I sell the house? . . . I want all the children . . . Why should I send my children into that kind of an atmosphere?"

Megan had heard enough. She quietly climbed the stairs to her room, went inside, and closed the door. She pulled a blanket off the bed, went into her closet, sat down on the floor, and closed the door. She wrapped the blanket around her. She wished she were dead, but she didn't want to be dead if it caused her family any more grief. She wished that she could just cease to exist, that her name would be suddenly wiped from all the records in the world and nobody would ever remember she had ever existed.

This is all my fault, she thought to herself over and over again. *If I'd never been born, this never would have happened. I wish I were dead.*

She heard the door slam and heavy footsteps as Derek ran up the stairs. She knew he would go in his room, drop off his books, and then come knocking on her door. She didn't want him to see her this way, so she got up and threw the blanket back on the bed and wiped her eyes, then pulled out a book and sat down at the desk.

"Hey, what's going on in there?" he called out, pounding on her door.

"You can come in."

He barged in. "You can't believe what people are saying about me at school today."

"What?"

"That MacKenzie and me were really going at it under the table in Pizza Hut and that I hit Jason in the jaw in a big fight. It's so unfair. How was your day?"

"Okay, I guess."

He flopped down on her bed. "Hey, you didn't make your bed today! Does this mean you're human after all? I can't believe it. One of these days your room will look just like mine."

"You think so?"

"No, not really. To get it that bad takes a special genius. What are you studying?"

She had to look at the book to find out. "American history."

"Ask me any question about American history," he challenged.

"What is Manifest Destiny?"

"Beats me."

"I don't know either," Megan said.

"Oh, wow, what's happening here? I can't believe it. I'm starting to rub off on you. One of these days you'll be known as the rebel of your school."

She wanted to tell him how bad she felt. She was pretty

sure he'd listen to her, but how could she begin to tell him or anyone that she wished she was no longer alive? Besides, she knew she would never try to kill herself, because that's not something she could ever imagine herself doing.

"You think you'd ever get into a fight?" he asked.

"No."

"Well, you never know. Jason still wants to fight me for fooling around with MacKenzie while he played video games. Well, if he does, I'm ready for him. Let me show you what to do if you ever do get into a fight. C'mon, stand up, we'll go a couple of rounds."

"I have to study."

"C'mon, c'mon, this won't take very long. Okay, what's your best friend's name?"

"Jennifer."

"Okay, let's say I'm Jennifer and you decide to punch me out some day. Okay, now, the thing to do is watch the eyes. The eyes telegraph everything the rest of the body is going to do. Okay, put up your dukes."

"I'm never going to fight anybody."

"You never know. I mean, who would have ever thought you wouldn't make your bed one day? Things like that sneak up on you. One day it's not making your bed and the next day you beat up Jennifer and steal her guy. Okay, are you watching my eyes? Okay, try and throw a punch."

She halfheartedly tried to hit him.

"You're not watching my eyes. You got to watch the eyes . . ." He stopped speaking and his mouth dropped open. "You've been crying, haven't you!"

"No, I just got something in my eye on the way home from school."

"Both eyes?"

"No. Oh, Derek, I feel so bad."

She cried a long time. He didn't know what to say, so he

didn't say anything. He just let her cry. He touched her hand though.

"It's all my fault," she said.

"What is?"

"Mom and Dad breaking up. It's all my fault."

"Why is it your fault?"

"Because when I was born, they never had enough money after that."

"It's not your fault. It's not any of us kids' fault. It's Dad's fault because he looked at Gloria too much."

"I heard Mom talking to him. He wants Mom to sell the house and maybe split us up."

"That'll never happen."

"Mom was practically crying when she was talking to him. I felt so bad." She paused. "I wanted to . . . to give up."

Derek didn't understand what she meant. "You can't ever give up," he said.

"I know." She dried her eyes. "I'm all right now. Thanks for coming in."

"Hey, I'm always happy to come and bother people. The way I look at it, if I can keep you from studying, then you won't get such good grades, and that'll make me look better."

"I'm glad you stopped in to see me," she said.

"You are? No kidding? I always thought I was pretty much a pain to you."

"Sometimes you are, but not always. Especially not today."

"I did something right today then. Wow, I've gotta go write that down in my journal." He paused at the door. "If I can find my journal, that is."

"I'm glad you're my brother," she said.

He cleared his throat awkwardly and, in a barely audible voice, said, "Thanks." He wiped his eyes. "You're pretty okay too. Now that Dad's gone, we have to stick together. Well, I guess I'll go down and make myself a peanut butter sandwich. See you later."

He paused on the staircase and shouted, "Megan is glad I'm her brother!" And then he thundered down the stairs as usual.

When Kimberly got home from school the next day, her mother was resting on her bed.

"Anything wrong?" Kimberly asked.

"Just a headache, that's all. I tried to find a job again today."

"How'd it go?"

"I should have finished college."

"Why didn't you?"

"I got married young and then got pregnant soon after."

"With me."

"Yes, but that's not the problem. I should have been taking classes every year since then, but at the time I couldn't see any need to graduate. Now I do. Basically I can get the same kind of job now that I could have had when I was a senior in high school. Minimum-wage jobs. One thing's for sure, we're going to have to cut way back on the way we live."

"Dad should pay for everything. It's his fault this is happening anyway."

"He's willing to pay child support, but that won't cover everything."

Ben showed up a few minutes later, and he and Kimberly went downstairs to practice some songs.

"I might not be able to practice as much anymore," she told him.

"Why not?"

"I've got to get a job to help out my family."

"If we want to keep our job at Angelo's, we've got to practice."

"I know that, but maybe not so much."

"What kind of a job do you have in mind?"

"I'm not sure. I think I'll check around campus and see what's available."

At two in the morning, Derek got up to go to the bathroom. Then he went downstairs to the kitchen and dialed Gloria's phone number. When she answered, he hung up and went back to his room.

Just as he closed the door to his room, he heard the phone ring. He went to the top of the stairs to listen in. His mother answered it in her room on the first floor. "No, there's nobody up now. Why?" he heard her say.

Derek hopped back in bed. He heard his mother coming up the stairs and then going into the bathroom. A short time later she opened his door. "Derek?" she whispered.

He pretended to be asleep.

"Derek, I need to talk to you." She shook him gently. "Wake up."

"What?"

"Your dad just phoned me. Somebody just called Gloria and hung up when she answered. She was upset so she called your father at his apartment and then he called me, wanting to know if it was any of us. I told him I'd find out. Derek, was it you?"

"No, I've been asleep."

"Are you sure?"

"Yes."

"I heard the toilet flush a few minutes ago. Was that you?"

"No."

"Are you sure? The seat was up so it wasn't Kimberly or Megan. I need to know if it's you that's been calling Gloria and hanging up."

After several seconds, he said, "I might have done it a few times."

"I can understand you being mad at Gloria, but this isn't doing anybody any good."

"It makes me feel better."

"Would you like to tell your father yourself how angry you are at what he's done?"

"No."

"Why not?"

"He'd just give me a lecture."

"What if he promised not to do that? What if he promised just to listen to what you have to say?"

"It wouldn't make any difference. He'd still turn it around so everything is my fault."

"What if I was there to keep him from doing that?"

"Would he let you tell him why you're so mad at him?"

"No, I don't think he'd let me do that."

"Well, if he won't do it for you, then I don't want him to do it for me."

"There's a difference. He may not always be my husband, but he will always be your father."

"I don't want him for a father anymore."

"He still loves you."

"No, he doesn't. He's never liked me very much."

"How can you say that?"

"It's true. He's never been satisfied with anything I've ever done."

"You should have heard him brag to people how smart you were."

"He never told me that."

"I'm sorry he didn't." She touched his sleeve. "He's so proud that you're about to get your Eagle."

"I'm not getting it."

"I understand how you feel, but don't give up on it now." She paused, then said, "Derek, do you know how much I love you?"

"Not really."

She put her hand on his shoulder. "You're the most wonderful son anyone could ever have."

Derek stook up and moved to the window so his mother couldn't see him wiping his eyes. "Thanks, Mom."

She went to him and gave him a big hug. He was no longer her little boy; already he towered over her. "You're getting to be so tall and strong, but it's okay for you to come and talk to me when you feel bad. Okay?"

"Okay." He let her hold him longer than usual and then moved away.

"Well, we'd both better get back to sleep. Good night. No more crank phone calls, okay?"

"Okay."

The next day Anne waited until supper to tell her family what she considered to be good news. "Guess what, kids — I got a job! I start tomorrow."

"Where at?"

"Jiffy Buns Donut Shop. It doesn't pay much, but at least it's a job. I'll work early mornings and whenever someone else can't make it. It means you're all going to have to get ready for school without me. Oh, there's one other thing. Derek, I need to talk to you after supper."

After supper Anne had a private conversation with Derek in her bedroom.

"I talked to your father today. I told him I thought you needed to express your feelings to him. He agreed to come over tonight and let you tell him how you're feeling about all this."

"I'm not talking to him."

"I can understand why you feel that way. Look, if you want I'll be in the same room to make sure he doesn't intimidate you."

"Why do I have to do it if I don't want to?"

"Calling Gloria in the middle of the night and then hanging up is not a very grown-up way of expressing anger."

"Did you tell him about that?" Derek asked.

89

"Yes, I did. It's better they know it was you rather than worry that it might be some homicidal maniac on the loose."

"I can't talk to him."

"What are you afraid of?"

"That he'll turn it all around and make it out that we were the ones who messed up. I can hear him saying, 'If you kids had only kept the house cleaner, then this would never have happened.'"

"A man doesn't abandon his wife and kids because the house isn't as clean as he'd like it to be."

"He'll end up lecturing me like he always does."

"I'll make sure he doesn't do that. Look, if it's too awful, you can always get up and walk out on him."

He paused. "I can?"

"Yes."

"Okay."

"He said he'd be here at about eight."

A little before eight Derek saw his father's car drive up but his father didn't get out of his car until it was precisely eight o'clock. Anne let him in, then called up the stairs, "Derek, your father is here."

Derek went down to the kitchen, where his father sat at the table. He stood up as Derek came in. "Hello, Derek."

"Hello," Derek said, trying to sound like a computer. They both sat down. His mother was sitting on a bar stool in the corner of the room.

In some ways his father looked like he usually did, except somehow it was different. It was as if somehow he'd lost his authority as a father. "How are you coming on completing your requirements for Eagle?" he began.

Derek couldn't believe it. Later, when he told Kimberly about the interview, he said, "The man leaves his wife for some stupid secretary, and the first thing he does is ask me how close I am to becoming an Eagle scout."

90

Derek was furious with the question but tried not to show it. "All right."

"When do you think you'll get it?"

"I don't know."

"If you ever need any help on your Eagle project, just let me know."

"Yeah, sure."

"Your mother says you didn't go to scouts last week. You're so close to Eagle now. Don't stop now just because you're mad at me."

"Why do you want me to get it? So you can impress Gloria with what a great dad you are?"

There was a long, awkward silence, and then his father said, "Why don't you go ahead and tell me everything you're feeling about me these days?"

Derek knew his mother had suggested the question, because it was not a question his father had ever asked anybody.

"Not good."

"Why's that?"

"I don't see why you had to leave us."

"That is between your mother and me. Let me assure you that it's not because I suddenly quit loving my children."

"No, it's because you suddenly started loving your secretary."

"What else would you like to share with me?"

"Not a thing."

"Are you sure?"

"Yes. What good would it do anyway?"

His father waited a few seconds and then said, "All right. While we're here, I think we should talk about these crank phone calls you've been making. I hope you realize that what you've been doing is against the law. I could notify the police about this, and I will if it keeps up. In fact, I checked into it. It's actually a federal offense, and the FBI can be involved in cases like these."

Derek was furious. He stood up. "Can I go now? I have to go work on scouting. I want to get my Eagle so I can make you proud of me."

Anne intervened. "Derek, don't leave. We're not done here. Paul, this has been totally unsatisfactory. You waltz in here, barely pay any attention to Derek, and then proceed to tell him you're going to turn him over to the FBI."

"He said he didn't have anything else to say to me. What was I supposed to do? Besides, don't I have any rights in this matter? You don't know how upset Gloria gets every time she answers the phone and nobody's there."

"Why don't you listen to your son for once in your life?"

"All right, Anne, now calm down. If you're not careful, you'll give yourself another migraine."

"Don't be patronizing, Paul."

"I wasn't being patronizing. I was just stating a fact of life. You do get migraines."

"Not since you left." It wasn't true, but she said it just to get back at him.

Paul glanced at his watch. The gesture was not lost on Anne. "Oh dear, Paul, I do hope we're not wasting your valuable time." She looked at him with mock sympathy, then added, "You know, I can't believe you. This is your only son. You do remember that, don't you?"

"If he has something to say, then why doesn't he say it?"

Derek felt like a tennis ball being batted back and forth. He couldn't take it anymore. He stalked out of the room and up the stairs to his room and slammed the door as hard as he could.

He could hear his mother and father downstairs arguing. And then after a while his father left.

Most of that night Megan stayed at her desk, working on a map that was due in the morning. It was to be a map of Utah. Her teacher had given her a list of fifty geographical sites to

92

be included on the map. She had given specific guidelines: rivers were to be blue, interstates red, towns over fifty thousand orange.

Megan felt like she would either get an A or a B on the map. She knew it was important to be neat and accurate. She had been working on the map for several days.

She was just finishing it up when her father came. She opened her door to listen. She could hear the muffled sounds of Derek and her father going after each other, followed by Derek stalking up the stairs and slamming the door. And then her mother and father were yelling at each other in the kitchen.

Megan took out a pair of scissors and folded the map neatly into fourths and cut along the creases. She then took each of the fourths and cut them into fourths. She repeated it again and again until all that was left of the map was dozens of small, precisely cut pieces.

9

Two days later Kimberly announced after supper that she also had found a job.

"Where?" her mother asked.

"Working for one of the professors in my department. He's got a research project, and he needs someone to help out. It's mostly routine things, you know—cleaning up, taking data, things like that—but it pays six dollars an hour."

"When will you work?" Ben asked.

"After classes three days a week. I'll be done by six o'clock. And there's a possibility I might be able to work this summer full-time. Isn't that great?"

"Sounds terrific," her mother said. "Where do I sign on? It's more than I'm making."

"At least I'll be able to help out now."

"They're paying you to do research?" Derek asked. "What a mistake. You'll probably blow up the lab."

"That's really great you've got a job," Ben said.

"Yes, and we can work on music the other two days a week."

Megan finished brushing her teeth and then found herself looking at her reflection in the mirror. She wondered how it was that nobody seemed to know how bad she felt. Sometimes it was okay, sometimes she even felt good, but then, even only a few minutes later, she would descend into a black hole, and there didn't seem to be any way out.

She must have lost track of time, because suddenly she heard Derek banging on the door. "Megan, what's the big delay here? There are other people in this family, you know. What do you want me to do, go outside?"

She opened the door.

"After I leave home, I'll never share a bathroom with another female," Derek complained. "You and Kimberly drive me crazy. Before you get married, I'm going to have a talk with your future husband and tell him how much time you take in here. If he's smart, he'll build himself his own private bathroom. Otherwise he's going to spend his whole life waiting for you to get out of the bathroom."

She smiled. "Oh yeah? Well, I've got one or two things to tell the girl you marry, so you'd better watch out."

"Me? What could you possibly tell about me?"

"Right, I forgot, you're perfect. Goodnight, Derek."

A week later Anne called her family together. "I'm sorry, kids, but there's something else we need to talk about. Even with what Dad will be giving us each month and with me and Kimberly working, there's not going to be enough money coming in. We have to be very careful about how we spend our money from now on."

"Why don't you just ask Dad to give you more?" Megan asked.

"All that has been turned over to our lawyers. My lawyer says that with Dad being willing to give us the house, it might be very hard to get more for child support. If I want to earn more money than what I'm making at Jiffy Buns, I might need to finish college."

"But won't it cost a lot of money to do that?" Megan asked.

"Yes, but after I graduate, I'll be able to make a decent salary, so it'll pay off in the long run. It'll mean taking night

95

classes occasionally, and having to study sometimes when you'd rather have me take you to the mall."

"If we're not making it now, how are you going to pay for college?" Derek asked.

"That's what we need to talk about. I talked it over with your father. He suggested I sell the house. That would give us some extra money. It would also help Kimberly and me pay for college next year. So selling the house has some advantages. What would you think about it?"

"Where would we live?" Derek asked.

"We'd either rent a house or an apartment."

"With a pool?" Megan asked.

"Yes, maybe we could even find an apartment with a pool."

"Just make Dad give us more money," Derek said.

"I wish it were that easy. Kimberly, what do you think?"

"Well, if it would make things easier for us in the long run, maybe we should do it."

"What if we sell the house and end up crammed all together in a tiny apartment?" Derek asked.

"We'd have to make sure that didn't happen. Would you object if we find out how much we can get for our house?"

"I guess not," Derek said.

"Megan?" Anne asked.

"Sure, it won't hurt to find out."

Anne decided to put the house on the market, ask for more than she expected she could get for it, and then take her time to see if that's really what they should do. She announced that on Saturday the entire family would work to get it clean enough to show to buyers.

Ben and Brother Hatch volunteered to put in new linoleum in the upstairs bathroom. On Saturday they showed up at nine and began taking out the old linoleum.

Derek worked for a while, then went across the hall to Megan's room. He sat on her bed and watched her sort through some things in her closet.

"Look what I found," she said, handing him a stuffed bear she'd gotten at Yellowstone Park on vacation the summer before.

"Nice bear. Does it have a name?"

"Buffy."

"Buffy the Bear. Hello, Buffy the Bear."

"Remember we got it at Fishing Bridge? I wanted it but Mom said I already had plenty of stuffed animals. Then Dad said it would be all right and he got it for me."

"What a great dad, right? I wonder if he liked Gloria then. If he did, I bet he could hardly wait to get back to work."

"You don't have to wreck all my memories, do you?"

"Sorry. Are you going to keep Buffy the Bear?"

"No, I guess not."

"So long, Buffy." He slam-dunked the bear into the trash bag.

"Don't treat him so mean." She pulled the bear out of the trash bag.

"I'd better get back to work. Take care of Buffy for me, okay?"

Derek went to Kimberly's room to see how she was doing in cleaning up her room. She was almost done.

"Is it okay if I come in?" he asked.

"Sure. You can even help by carrying this stuff I'm throwing away outside."

She had three large trash bags full of junk. He took them outside. When he returned, he said, "It only took me one trip. Aren't you impressed?"

"I always knew you'd be a good garbage man," she said.

"You'd be the first thing I'd haul away."

"Yeah, yeah."

She had found an old candy bar in a box. "Here, I saved this for you."

"How old is it?"

"At least a year."

97

"Just right." He tore open the wrapper and took a bite. "So when are you and Ben going to make a million dollars in the music world?"

She smiled. "After we work a million hours."

"If some big recording company wants to do an album, put me on the cover, okay? People will buy it just for the picture of me."

"Do you realize you're the only conceited one in our family?" Kimberly asked.

"Maybe so, but do you realize that I'm the only one in the family who has any reason to be conceited?"

She threw a pillow at him.

After Megan finished with her room, she went to talk to Ben and Brother Hatch. She looked around. The old linoleum had been ripped out and the toilet was in the hall.

"You think we'll ever be able to use this room again?"

"Probably not," Ben joked.

"He's right, Megan," Brother Hatch said. "I hope you're good friends with your neighbors, because we're going to tear into the downstairs bathroom next."

"You'll fix this one first though, won't you?"

"I don't know. What do you think?" Brother Hatch said.

"Fix one before you wreck 'em both."

"Gosh, that's a good idea, Megan. We're glad you came along, aren't we, Ben?"

"Sure, Megan's good to have around, even if she is mean to me," Ben said.

"I'm not mean to you."

"You're supposed to have a crush on me, Megan."

"What for?"

"Because I'm older and wiser."

"Brother Hatch is even older and wiser, and I don't have a crush on him."

"You don't?" Brother Hatch asked in a shocked voice before laughing.

"See what I mean?" Ben said. "She's a heartbreaker."

"But we love her all the same, don't we?" Brother Hatch said. "Megan, how are things going with you?"

"In school, you mean?"

"No. With *you*."

"All right, I guess."

"You want to talk about anything?"

"Not really."

"Now's your big chance. Ben and I aren't going anywhere for a while."

She thought for a moment and then said, "I don't understand adults."

"What don't you understand?"

"My dad knew it wasn't right to fall in love with someone else, so why did he do it if he knew it was wrong?"

"Things like this happen a little at a time, and going from one step to the other doesn't usually seem all that bad," Brother Hatch said.

"People keep saying I'm turning into a woman, and I know things are happening, but sometimes I get afraid."

"What are you afraid of?" Ben asked.

"That I'll end up doing things I know are wrong but I won't be able to stop because it'll take over my life. I mean, that's what happened to my dad, isn't it? Something just took over. I'm not sure I want to be an adult. Maybe I won't be able to control myself the way my dad can't control himself. I mean, how else can you explain why he would just walk away from us?"

"Things just don't take over your life unless at some point in the beginning you give them permission," Ben said.

"I don't like it when people tell me how fast I'm growing up." She paused. "Ben, I don't like it when you tell me that if things don't work out with Kimberly, you're going to come for me."

"I'm sorry, Megan, I just meant I think you're a wonderful girl. I won't say it anymore."

"I don't want to talk about it anymore either," she said.

She watched them work for a few minutes and then returned to her room. She cleaned a spot on Buffy the Bear and carefully packed him in a box of things to be saved.

On the next Saturday they had a garage sale. Anne had to work, and so she asked Kimberly to be in charge. The sale wasn't supposed to start until eight-thirty, but people started showing up at seven. By eleven o'clock most of the good stuff was gone. It started to rain in the afternoon, but it didn't make any difference because by then they had sold most of it anyway. Megan was in charge of keeping track of the money. She proudly announced they had made $267.23.

On Tuesday of the next week, after supper, the phone rang. It was for Anne. When she got off the phone, she told the family that the realtor was bringing someone over to see the house, so they needed to hurry through the house and pick up everything.

"It's like we have to be this ideal family spending a wonderful evening at home," Derek said.

"We need a dad, though," Kimberly said. "Come with me and we'll get one."

Kimberly, Derek, and Megan went into the attic and found an inflatable clown. Megan blew it up. Derek found one of their father's old hats and put it on top of the clown's head. Then they put the clown on a chair in front of the kitchen table with a newspaper propped up in front of it. They started laughing so hard that Anne came in to see what was going on. She made them put it all away.

Ten minutes later the real estate agent arrived with a man and his wife. They walked through the house like nobody was there, with the man criticizing everything he saw. For every complaint the real estate agent said, "We can take care of that."

After they left, Derek went to his mother to complain. "I don't like people walking through our house. I don't like it at all."

"Nobody does, but it's one of the things you have to put up with when you're trying to sell a house."

"Dad gets a younger woman, and we get strangers walking through our house."

"Here it is," Anne said the next day as they pulled into a parking space next to the brick apartment building.

"This dump?" Derek said.

"I'm not saying we'll take it. It's just one we can look at to see what they're like."

"I don't want to live here," Megan said.

"C'mon, you guys," Kimberly said. "Don't be so negative all the time. The least we can do is look at it."

They got a key from the manager and walked up two flights of stairs. The door to the apartment opened into the kitchen. It had a lonely echo.

"I know it's not as nice as we'd like, but if we worked on it, we could fix it up," their mother said.

"Where would we all sleep?" Megan asked.

"I was thinking Kimberly and Megan could be in one bedroom and Derek in the other."

"What about you?" Kimberly asked.

"We could get a couch that makes into a bed, and I could sleep on it in the living room."

"Why do we have to move anyway?" Derek asked.

"We don't have to. It's just that if we were to sell the house, we'd have more money to live on and pay for school expenses."

"There's a spider in the tub," Megan said, coming out of the bathroom.

"It comes with the apartment," Derek said sarcastically.

"Look, you guys," Kimberly said, "I don't think you should be so negative about everything. Mom's is doing the best she can. If we all work together, we can make things work out."

"You want my opinion?" Derek said. "Okay, here it is. I say we stay in our house and never move."

There was silence, followed by Megan saying, "I don't see why we have to move either."

"If we don't sell the house, I don't see how I can go to college," Anne pointed out.

"I think it's too late for you to go to college," Derek said. "You should have done that when you were Kimberly's age."

Anne sighed. "Let's go home."

That night Megan went into Derek's room. "Did you know that Mom was crying when she drove us home?"

"So?"

"You shouldn't have told her it was too late for her to go to college."

"Hey, she asked, so I told her what I thought. What else am I supposed to do?"

10

The next day there was no school because it was an in-service day for teachers. Anne had to work all day, but she made a list of things that needed to be done by the family before she got home.

Between her classes at the university, Kimberly took charge of getting Megan and Derek to help with the work. It took almost all morning. Just before lunch, she approached Derek. "There's one more thing Mom wanted us to do today."

"What?"

"Go to the scout office and pick up an application for your Eagle service project. Ben's coming over soon to take us there."

"Forget it."

"Derek, you're so close to getting your Eagle. All you have to do is your project and a little paperwork. Don't quit now."

"The only reason I even got started in scouts was because of Dad."

"So now you're going to give up what you've been working on for so long?"

"Yes, that's right. I'm through."

"It's not just that Dad wants you to get it. Mom does and so do I. I've never had a brother who was an Eagle scout before."

"No, I'm done with all that."

"Look, Mom made me promise I'd take you to the scout

office so you could pick up an application. Once we get that done, we're both off the hook and can do whatever we want the rest of the afternoon. So let's get it over with, okay?"

By the time Ben arrived and picked them up, the scout office was closed for the noon hour. "I'd like to go shopping for some clothes over at the mall," Kimberly said. "You two interested?"

"I am," Ben said.

"Not me," Derek said. "I think I'll sit on the grass and listen to a tape MacKenzie lent me."

"All right, we'll meet you back here at one o'clock. Okay?"

"Yeah, sure."

Derek sat on the grass of a park across the street from the scout office and listened to music on a Walkman he'd bought. At ten minutes to one he glanced up and saw a woman opening the door. By the time he crossed the street and entered the building, the woman was on the phone in another office answering a question about the whittling merit badge. Derek stood and waited. On the counter was an Eagle medallion in a felt-covered black box.

If Dad wants an Eagle, maybe I should give him one, he thought. *He could hang it on the wall of his office, and then when people came, he could tell everyone what a wonderful father he was because his son had his Eagle. Yes, I should do this for Dad. He wants me to get an Eagle so much and we don't ever want to disappoint our father even though he disappoints us all the time and then in the end he leaves us all without enough money and no way for any of us to ever climb out of the hole he's left us in.*

He grabbed the box, stuffed it in his shirt, checked to make sure the woman hadn't seen him, looked around to be sure nobody was coming in the office, and slipped quietly out the door and went across the street. Then he opened the box, removed the medallion and stuffed it in the front pocket of his jeans, and hid the black box in his windbreaker. He

104

walked over to a nearby dumpster and got rid of the box, then returned to the park bench.

While he waited for Kimberly and Ben to return, he tried to imagine how he would give the medallion to his father. Maybe he'd hang it on the antenna of his dad's car, or maybe he'd put it under one of the tires so that when his father pulled out, it would give him a flat tire. Or maybe he'd send it to Gloria with a note that read, "You deserve this more than I do." Or maybe he'd nail it to the door of Gloria's apartment so his father would see it the next time he went to her apartment. *If he wants an Eagle,* Derek thought, *then I'll make sure he gets one. We must always do what our father tells us to do, even when our father is a hypocrite and a liar and can't ever be trusted again.*

He knew Kimberly wouldn't let him leave until he'd picked up the application form, so he would have to go back to the office. He would have to be careful what he said. He decided he would need to appear eager to earn his Eagle so they wouldn't suspect him.

The first question Kimberly asked when she and Ben returned was if he'd gotten the application form yet. He yawned and stretched. "No, not yet."

"Well, c'mon, let's get this over with so we can have the rest of the afternoon free."

Just as they approached the door, a man who worked at the scout office returned from lunch and opened it for them. "Can I help you?" he asked.

"My brother needs an application for his Eagle service project," Kimberly responded.

The man was chatty and pleasant. He introduced himself as Art Gulbransen and said he was the local scout executive. He took Derek's name and address and asked about his progress. Derek tried to be positive and cheerful so Mr. Gulbransen would not be suspicious of him when they discovered the medallion was missing.

105

On the way home, Kimberly asked Derek about the change in his attitude when he had been talking to the scout executive.

"I was thinking, maybe you're right. Maybe I should finish when I'm this close," he told her.

"Mom will be so proud of you. And so will I."

"But especially Dad will, right? I mean, we've got to make Dad proud, don't we?"

She looked at him strangely but didn't say anything.

That night Mr. Gulbransen phoned Derek. "I was wondering if you saw anything suspicious this afternoon when you came in to pick up the application form."

Derek's heart raced. "What do you mean by suspicious?"

"I'm not sure. Someone said they saw a boy across the street during the noon hour. Was that you?"

"Yes, that was me."

"How long were you there?"

"About thirty minutes."

"Did you notice anyone going into the scout office during that time?"

"No, but I wasn't watching. And I did take a little walk around the park. Why do you ask?"

"One of our Eagle medallions has turned up missing."

"Could it have been misplaced?"

"That's not likely. We had it set out on the counter for someone to pick up. We noticed it was gone around two o'clock. You don't know what happened to it, do you?"

"No."

"I just thought I'd check to see if you saw anything suspicious. If it were returned right away, we wouldn't contact the police."

"I hope you don't think I took it."

"No, not really. It doesn't make sense for someone as close as you are to Eagle to steal one. But I'm afraid I'm going to

106

have to contact the police about this. Whoever did this needs to learn that crime doesn't pay."

"Scouting teaches that."

"Yes, of course it does. Well, I'm sorry to have bothered you. We're all looking forward to the time when you finish your Eagle project. When will that be?"

"I'll be done in a month."

"Well, good luck with everything. Good night."

Derek hung up the phone. He had difficulty breathing. His forehead was beaded with sweat. He felt that Mr. Gulbransen suspected him but didn't have any evidence that he'd been the one who had stolen the Eagle medallion.

He thought about taking Mr. Gulbransen's offer and admitting that he was the one who'd done it. The only problem with that was that his mother would find out, and Derek wasn't sure she could take that on top of everything else that was happening in the family. Besides, if he didn't tell, there was no way they could ever find out for sure.

He decided that the best way to keep Mr. Gulbransen from suspecting him was to go ahead and finish his requirements for Eagle. He went downstairs to talk to his mother. "I've decided to try and finish up my requirements for Eagle as soon as I can."

She smiled. "That's wonderful, Derek. We're all so proud of you."

He went to his room and closed the door and tried to deal with the guilt that now pressed down on him from every side.

11

Ben sat behind Kimberly with his arms wrapped around her waist as they gazed out at the lights of the city. It was a Saturday night, and they had just come to his apartment from working at Angelo's.

His aunt came up the stairs. "I hope you like lots of butter on your popcorn, because that's the way I fixed it."

"Thanks a lot," Ben said.

"I'll just set it here on the table. Are you two still looking out the window?"

"I never get tired of it," Kimberly said.

"I'll leave the door open, if that's all right," she said as she left.

"It's great having your aunt on duty," Kimberly said with a slight smile.

Ben kissed her on the back of the neck.

"I don't know how you can stand me when I smell like a pizza," Kimberly whispered.

"I like pizza," he said, kissing her neck again.

She laughed. "Yes, I can see that you do."

He untangled himself and went to his desk. "I bought a surprise for you today. Close your eyes." He placed a small box in a sandwich bag, set it in a small bowl, and dumped some popcorn over it. "Okay, you can open your eyes." He handed her the bowl.

"Have some popcorn."

"I'm not really that hungry."

"Please."

She reached in for the popcorn and felt the bag.

"What's going on here?" Inside the box she found an engagement ring.

"Will you marry me?" Ben asked.

"Oh, my gosh! I wasn't expecting this! Are you sure you want to give me this?"

"Kimberly, I love you. I can't stand the thought of not spending the rest of eternity with you. Yes, I'm sure. I talked to my aunt and she said we could stay here so you'd be close to your family, and we could even send them a little money every month. And we could still work at Angelo's on the weekends. We can be married in the temple, and everything will be just the way we want it." He put his arms around her and kissed her. "And one other thing. We'd be here every night, just the two of us. And we'd finally be able to close the door at the bottom of the stairs."

She stood up and walked around the room, turning on all the lights. "I don't know what to say. My mind is racing. We'd stay here? Is it big enough for two of us? What's the bedroom like? Do you mind if I look in?"

"Go ahead. I made the bed today."

She opened the bedroom door. "This is a really small room. We'd need a mirror above my vanity for when I put on makeup. Can you do that?" she asked.

"I'm Mister Hardware Man, remember? I can do anything. I'd just get some quarter-inch-long toggle bolts. Take about two minutes."

She stuck her head out of the bedroom. "Toggle bolts, huh? We'd also need more closet space."

"No problem. With a little planning we can double the amount of closet space available.

She went over to the tiny kitchen area. "We'd need more cupboard space. And one of the burners doesn't work."

"I know. It needs replacing."

"This is fun being domestic!"

"With you it is."

"Ben, there's one thing you need to understand. I really do want to finish college."

"I think you should."

"I still don't know what to say. I think maybe my family might be able to get along without me. I mean, Derek's doing okay—he's getting his Eagle soon. And Megan seems to be doing well. So maybe it would be okay for me to leave. Does this offer of yours have an expiration date?"

"You mean like on a carton of milk? No, not really."

"Just give me some time to think about it, okay?"

"Sure. Do you have any idea how much I love you?" he said.

"I love you too. I really do, but right now, tell me again about the closets."

He held her in his arms and whispered step by step how he was going to double the closet space.

Kimberly woke her mother up when she came in from being with Derek. The first thing she did was tell about Ben's proposal. "What do you think I should do?" she asked.

"What do you want to do?"

"I really love him and I want to marry him."

"Then I think you should. You couldn't find a more wonderful man than Ben."

"I know. He's been so good for me. Do you think I should wait a while before I get married?"

"Oh, I don't know. You're the same age I was when I married your father." There was a long, awkward silence. "I guess that's not such a great recommendation anymore, is it?"

110

"And what about my leaving the family now? I feel like I should stick around for Derek and Megan."

"You can't live on shoulds. What do *you* want?"

She thought about it. "I want to spend my life with Ben."

"Then why don't you tell him that?"

"I will, but in my own special way next Saturday night."

"Thank you very much," Kimberly said after the two of them finished a song for appreciative patrons in the restaurant on Saturday evening. "Our next song is one we worked on in January but never finished. But as a surprise for Ben, I've finished it. I'd like to dedicate it to him tonight because this is a special night for the two of us. Ben, this is your song."

She did a short introduction on the guitar and then, gazing into his eyes, began singing:

A fireplace hearth on a wintry night,
Your face aglow in the firelight.
Do you remember? I really do,
How, for you, in those embers my love grew.

An April night, a window for two,
You asked me if I would marry you.
Could you forget? Well, I never will,
For I'll be yours, in love, forever.

She ended the song, then shouted, "Yes, Ben, I'll marry you!"

The crowd caught on to what was happening before Ben did. Some clapped and yelled. Finally Ben realized what had happened. He threw his arms around Kimberly and kissed her, to the delight of everyone there.

That night after everyone else had gone to bed, Kimberly looked at her mother's wedding pictures. Her mother had

111

been a beautiful bride, standing in front of the Salt Lake Temple with her new husband.

Kimberly suddenly wondered how anyone could have possibly known then that her parents' marriage was going to end in divorce. *I'm not ready for this,* she thought, experiencing a sudden feeling of panic and dread.

12

The next Tuesday, while Derek was studying in his room, the doorbell rang. A minute later his mother called for him. "Derek?"

"What?"

"There's a police officer here who would like to talk to you."

Derek's heart raced and his breathing became labored. His first impulse was to run, but he knew he couldn't do that. He walked down the stairs. An older man in a police uniform stood at the bottom.

"I just need a few minutes of your time," the man said. "I'm looking into the theft of the Eagle medallion from the scout office."

"Don't you have more important things to worry about?"

"Actually, I'm doing this off-duty. You see, I'm an Eagle scout myself. Mr. Gulbransen asked me to do some investigating, not so much because of the value of the medallion, but to see if we can help whoever stole it."

"You think I stole it?"

"Not at all. It's just that, as I understand it, you were at the scout office about the time it was stolen. Is that right?"

Derek felt there was a trap in anything the policeman said. "I have no idea when it was stolen, so I can't say I was there when it was stolen."

"You were across the street before the office opened at one o'clock. Is that right?"

"Yes."

"Why were you there?"

"My sister Kimberly and Ben — he's the guy she's going to marry — brought me, but when we got there, the office was closed. Kimberly wanted to go shopping and I decided to sit in the park. It was a nice day, and I had a new tape I wanted to listen to. So I just waited there until they came back, and then we went and got what I needed."

"Is Kimberly at home now?"

"Yes."

"May I speak to her?"

The policeman spoke privately to Kimberly, then thanked them both and left.

Derek went to his room. Kimberly knocked and asked if she could come in. When she entered, he was pacing the floor. "How long are they going to keep coming back and asking the same questions over and over? I told them I don't know anything about it. Why do they keep coming back if it's not because they think I did it?"

"I think you're overreacting. You didn't do anything wrong, so you don't have anything to worry about. I told the policeman I was absolutely certain that you weren't the one who took it, so relax, okay?"

"I want to finish this stupid Eagle project so they'll know it wasn't me and they won't keep coming back. You've got to help me. I can't seem to get anything done. I can't even make the phone calls I'm supposed to make. I pick up the phone and then I freeze and think, what difference does it make? They already think I'm the one who stole the medallion. They won't ever let me have a moment's peace until I prove to them once and for all that I'm not the one who took the Eagle. Please help me. I can't do this by myself. Please, you've got to help me."

"Take it easy, okay? Sure, I'll help you. And we can get Ben to help too. We can work on it right now, if you want. Let's get this done once and for all."

True to her word, Kimberly and Ben helped Derek finish his Eagle project. It took a great deal of preparation and planning over the next two weeks, but it was completed in a day.

The first week in May, when Derek walked into the Eagle board of review, he was surprised to see Mr. Gulbransen there representing the scout office. Through everyone else's questions, Mr. Gulbransen said nothing. But then after everyone else was satisfied, he asked if he might ask Derek a few questions. "Derek, could you give us the scout law?"

"A scout is trustworthy . . . " He wiped his sweating forehead. He started coughing. Someone gave him a glass of water. "Thank you. . . . Uh, let's see, loyal, helpful, friendly, courteous, kind, obedient, cheerful, thrifty, brave, clean . . . and reverent."

"Very good. Can you tell us what trustworthy means?"

Derek knew his face was a bright red. "It means people can trust you."

"And are you trustworthy, Derek?" Mr. Gulbransen asked softly.

Derek knew that Mr. Gulbransen still suspected him. "Yes, I am."

Mr. Gulbransen looked at him for a long time and then nodded his head. "No other questions."

Derek passed his board of review.

"This is such a luxury," Anne said two days later as she had lunch at a restaurant with Kimberly.

"Thanks for thinking of the idea, Mom."

"I wanted you to know how much I appreciate what you've done to fill in for me the past few weeks. I lost track of a lot of things there for a while. Everything was so hard for me — getting used to working again, suffering from the loss of in-

115

come, having to cope with everything all by ourselves. Sometimes I wouldn't even notice what you were doing for Megan and Derek and me. I guess I was in shock there for a while. Anyway, I just wanted to let you know how much I appreciate what you've done. Thank you for going the extra mile. And now Derek's about to get his Eagle. And Megan seems like she's getting along okay. I'm getting used to my job. Things are looking up again for our family."

Kimberly smiled. She hoped her mother was right.

Derek sat on the stand and looked out into the chapel at the people who had come to see him become an Eagle scout. A Primary teacher from when he was little. A Sunday School teacher. The families who lived next door to them. In the front row were Kimberly and Ben, Megan, and his mother. His father was seated in the last row of the chapel. He had come just before the meeting began.

I've fooled them all, he thought. *I'm not trustworthy, I'm not cheerful, not anymore, not with this to worry about. I'm not brave, because if I was brave I would have told Mister Gulbransen the truth the first time he called. I'm not honest. I'm not clean—most of all I'm not clean.*

Looking at Megan made him feel worst of all because she looked up ˙ ɔ him, but now there wasn't anything worth looking up to.

Mr. Gulbransen came and sat on the stand. Then he leaned over and shook Derek's hand. Derek could hardly breathe. It was like a truck was parked on his chest. It did no good to look out into the audience, because everyone was looking at him like he was this wonderful person, and he knew the whole thing was a lie.

What made me think I could go through with this? he thought. *I can't do this. I think I'm going to die.*

During the opening song, he couldn't stand it anymore.

116

Suddenly he stood up and ran out of the building into the darkness of the night.

At first his family thought Derek would come home when he was tired of walking around. Anne stayed at home in case he called. Kimberly and Ben drove around in Ben's car, trying to find him. Paul took Megan with him, and they too drove around to places they thought Derek might go. Brother Hatch organized members of the high priests quorum into a search party to check the bus stations and shoulders along the interstate in case Derek was hitchhiking.

Ben and Kimberly called home every hour to see if Derek had been found yet. The rest of the time they drove past the homes of some of his friends.

At eleven o'clock, Kimberly turned to Ben. "It's getting late. You can take me home and go get some sleep if you want."

"No, that's okay. I'm not sleepy."

"You've been a good friend to Derek and Megan," she said. "I just want you to know that means a lot to me."

"It does to me too."

"I don't know how I would have made it without your help."

"We're in this together." He backed out of the parking place. "Where do you want to try now?"

"Let's drive by the school one more time."

Derek had walked around for a while and then doubled back to the church. He stayed in the shadows until only one car remained, and then quietly entered the building. He could see a light down the hall in the ward clerk's office. He ducked into a classroom and stayed there in the dark until he heard a car drive away, and then he came out and walked through the building without turning on any lights. The building creaked when the wind blew.

He tried to go into the chapel but it was locked. The doors

to the cultural hall were locked too, so he sat down on a couch in the foyer. The exit lights were the only lights on in the building. He thought about praying but decided against it. He was sure that God didn't want to hear from him again. That part of his life was over. He didn't want to ever come back to this building, didn't want to ever have to look in the faces of the younger scouts and know they were ashamed of him, didn't want to ever see his bishop, his Sunday School teacher, or his scoutmaster.

Since it didn't matter anymore what he did, he phoned MacKenzie from the hall phone. She answered. "This is Derek. I'd like to see you tonight," he said.

"I'm going with Jason."

"You can still go with Jason and see me once in a while too. Jason doesn't have to know. I could come by sometime when your parents aren't around, and we could fool around the way everyone thinks we did anyway. The way I see it, we've got nothing to lose, right?"

"I used to like you, Derek, but I don't anymore."

"Join the club. So, whattaya say, MacKenzie, you want me to come over tomorrow?"

She hung up.

He went back to the couch and sat down again. He felt that he had gone about as low as a person can go. *From now on,* he thought, *I'm on my own.*

He forced himself to think about Kimberly. He wished he never had to see her again, because he didn't want to see how much he had hurt her by living a lie. He knew he could have told her right away that he'd stolen the Eagle, and she would have gone in with him and talked Mr. Gulbransen out of calling the police. He knew she wouldn't have given up on him. The only thing that would make her give up on him was if he lied, and that's what he had done.

He looked around. Then he called out softly, "Hey, God,

118

here I am. If you want to strike me dead, go ahead. I don't care anymore."

Nothing happened. He felt like sleeping, but he knew he couldn't stay there forever. He had to go somewhere, but he couldn't go back home again. He didn't think he could face his family.

There was only one person he wasn't ashamed of seeing that night.

At about eleven o'clock her father dropped Megan off and then went out looking for Derek again. Her mother was downstairs waiting by the phone in case Derek called. Kimberly and Ben were still out looking.

Megan went up to her room and closed the door. She was certain that Derek had run away from home and would never come back, which meant she wouldn't even have him to talk to anymore.

She sat down at her desk. *I should write a note*, she thought. *You're supposed to write a note.* She opened her top drawer and pulled out two sheets of lined paper and began writing.

Dear Mom and Derek and Kimberly,

When you find this note, it will be too late. I love you all and I'm sorry for everything. Dad, I'm sorry about what happened the night you took me to the Ice Capades. If I'd said no when you first asked me, then our family would still be together. And I'm sorry that after I was born the family never had any money. I'm sorry things are so bad now. Just forget about me and everything will be all right.

Love,
Megan

She folded the note in two and taped it on her mirror. She wondered what it would be like to die. She hoped it would be like going to sleep and never waking up. *That would be the best if it's like that,* she thought. *But if it's like walking from one room into another, like some say, then that wouldn't be so good. I don't want to spend the rest of eternity having to explain why I ended my life. If only I knew what it's like.*

Their cat was scratching at her door. She got up and opened the door and let him in. The cat jumped up onto the bed and plopped himself on Megan's lap.

Tiger was his name. He liked to have his head petted, but nobody else in the family bothered much with that anymore. Megan hadn't done it for a long time, but because this would be her last chance, she did it. Tiger closed his eyes contentedly.

"You want to go outside now?" she asked a few minutes later. She picked Tiger up in her arms and went down the stairs to the back door. When she opened the door, Tiger hurried outside like someone late for an important meeting.

Megan decided to step outside. She wondered where Derek was and if he would ever come home again. It would be just like him to run away and never come back.

But if he comes back, she thought, *the first person he'll want to talk to will be me. I can't think about that. I just want to go to sleep and never wake up.*

She had hoped to see the stars one more time, because she loved to locate the Big Dipper and Orion. Derek had shown her how. But the sky was totally covered with clouds.

She felt a drop of rain land on her face. *I should go in,* she thought. But then she remembered it didn't matter anymore if she got a cold, so she decided to stay there and feel the rain coming down.

She closed her eyes. The rain was like a good friend coming to make things better. *What a wonderful thing for there to be rain,* she thought. *Soft and gentle, quiet and helpful. Instead of a gentle rain, what if God just took a huge bucket and dumped it on the earth? But that would scare the little children.*

120

This is so quiet that little boys and girls can sleep through it and never wake up.

Raindrops were trickling down her face. She opened her mouth and stuck out her tongue and captured some of the water and tasted it. Nothing had ever tasted so good.

She could see the outline of her rosebush in the family garden. Every year since she could remember, their family always had a garden. Last year they had divided the plot into thirds, and Megan and Kimberly and Derek each had responsibility for a section. They could plant anything they wanted. Derek planted corn and Kimberly planted radishes. But Megan planted a rosebush. It already had a tiny bud on it when they bought it. She had dusted it with rose dust to keep the bugs away, and watched it day after day as the bud unfolded into a beautiful, deep-red rose. Derek had teased her because at least what he was growing could be eaten, but Kimberly came to her rescue by telling him that the beauty of a rose feeds the spirit.

That happened last summer. And now another summer was coming, but she wouldn't be around to see it. She wondered how her rose would do this year. She couldn't imagine Derek or Kimberly or her mother dusting it to keep the bugs away. Everyone was too busy for that. She wondered if the rose would make it without her.

The intensity of the rain increased, and in a few minutes she was drenched. Tears started to come. She knew it didn't matter because her tears just mingled with the rain, and it would all help things grow. She went to her rosebush and knelt down and touched it. It was coming to life again for another summer. She felt the tiniest bud on one of the branches.

She thought about the rosebush, that even though it doesn't know if anyone is going to protect it against the bugs and hail or not getting watered, it still goes on making little buds every spring. And it never gives up, no matter what.

Suddenly she knew she didn't want to die, not even if things were bad in her family. They were bad, but the rosebush was still growing buds, and the rain was still coming down, and there would be a summer with hot days and swimming. How could she end her life when there's still rain to stand out in and cats to pet and roses to grow?

Her mother opened the door. "Megan?" she called out. She seemed desperate.

"I'm here, Mom."

"What are you doing?"

"I heard something. I thought it was Derek." Megan walked toward the house. "You're soaking wet."

"I know. Isn't it a wonderful rain?"

"Get out of your wet clothes right away before you catch a cold."

"I will. Have you heard from Derek yet?"

"Not yet."

"He'll come back."

"How do you know?"

"Because he and I need each other. Wake me up when he comes back. I know he'll want to talk. We're going to be all right, Mom, as long as there's rain."

She started up the stairs.

"Megan?"

"What?"

"I saw your note."

"You did?"

"Yes. I didn't know you were hurting so much. I promise you we'll find a way to make it better for you." She started to cry. "Oh, Megan, I couldn't bear to lose you."

Megan ran down the stairs and into her mother's arms.

Derek paused in front of the door to Gloria's apartment. It was past one o'clock in the morning. He knocked on the door for a long time before she opened it.

"Do you remember me? I'm Derek."

She let him in. "Everyone's out looking for you," she said.

"I know."

"Are you all right?"

"Yes."

"Can I fix you something to eat?"

"No."

"I can make some nachos."

"All right."

"And some salsa too?" she asked.

"Yes."

She fixed it, then watched him eat at the kitchen table. "Derek, I need to phone your mother and your father and tell them where you are. They need to know. They're really worried."

"Okay."

She made the phone calls and then came back to be with him.

"Some people don't think very much of you," he said.

"I know that."

"You knew my dad was married when you started liking him, didn't you?"

"Yes."

"Are you going to marry him after he gets divorced?"

"Yes."

"Are you ever going to have a baby?" he asked.

"We've talked about it."

"After you have your baby, will you keep working?"

"No, I'd probably quit work, at least until our child is old enough to be in school."

"So if you're not working, then maybe Dad will have to hire another secretary. Do you ever worry you'll end up like my mother?"

She faced him like a gunfighter unafraid of anything. "I

123

know this was hard for you, but we can't turn back what's already happened. We have to go on and do the best we can."

"That's what my mother is doing. She works at a donut shop. That's the best we can do right now. And here you are in a nice apartment. I'd say your best is better than our best."

"I've had this apartment for a long time. It has nothing to do with your father. I'm the one who pays the rent, not your father."

"How long have you been working for my father?"

"About a year and a half."

"A year and a half. That's all it took. I just don't understand what went wrong. If I could understand, then maybe it'd be better. You want to know something? I'm afraid I'll do the same thing to my wife."

"It's not hereditary, Derek. I wouldn't worry about it if I were you."

"I hope you don't mind my saying this, but you're not that great looking, if you ask me. I mean, you're pretty, but my mom, even though she's a lot older, looks okay when she gets dressed up."

"Yes, she's very attractive." She paused. "I often think about your mother."

"What about?"

"How she's doing. I'm sorry that she and I will probably never be friends."

"Friends? Are you crazy? She hates you. We all hate you. Did you purposely try to get my dad to go for you so he'd leave my mom?"

"No. We became friends first, then fell in love gradually. Do you have any other questions you want to ask me?"

"Would you answer any question I asked?"

"Yes, I think I owe you at least that. We're not going to get anywhere by putting walls up between us, are we?"

He sensed how tough she was, and that made him like her just a little bit more. "I guess I'm a lot like you now."

"How's that?"

"A disappointment to the people who used to respect me. I stole an Eagle medal from the scout office. Kind of a stupid thing to do, right?"

"We all make mistakes."

"I don't want to ever go back to church again," he said.

"Why not?"

"Because everyone is going to know what I did."

"They also will know you feel bad about it."

"Do you have any brothers?" he asked.

"No. Just one sister."

"Kimberly and Megan are my sisters."

"I know."

"Kimberly really helped me a lot with my Eagle project. She even told the police she was sure I wasn't the one who took the Eagle. I guess I fooled her, didn't I? I feel bad about that now. And then there's Megan. I like to go in her room and talk to her. She's always at her desk doing homework or some other dumb project. One time she told me she was glad I was her brother. We're really different though. She's so organized, and yet she likes me and even asks my advice sometimes." He paused. "I really think I'm the most like my dad of any of the kids."

"Why do you say that?"

"I can't be trusted either."

There was a knock on the door. Gloria opened the door, and Derek's father stepped in.

"We've all been worried sick about you," he said.

"Sorry."

Paul looked at his watch. "It's late. I'll take you home."

When Derek walked into the house, his mother ran over and gave him a hug. Kimberly did the same thing. Ben was there and gave him a pat on the back. Megan, hearing the noise, came running down the stairs.

"I stole the Eagle from the scout office."

"Yes, but we still love you," Kimberly said.

That was too much. Tears started down his face. Because he was embarrassed, he turned away.

Anne put her arms around him. Kimberly put her arm around his shoulder. Megan joined him on the other side and they held each other and let the tears come.

The next day Derek stayed home from school. He went with his mother to the scout office and confessed what he had done and gave back the medal he had stolen. Then he spent the afternoon writing letters of apology.

That night Brother Hatch and Mike came home teaching. Their lesson was on how our faith in the Savior can help us get through difficult times.

A day later Anne and her children met for the first time with a counselor in LDS Social Services. It was the first of four visits aimed at helping them communicate better as a family.

13

"Thank you for coming," Kimberly said when she opened the door to Ben two days later. She placed the engagement ring in his hand. "I need to give this back. Things are too crazy here now. I still love you, and everything, but I'm not ready to get married now. Not only that, I've got to be here for Megan and Derek. They need me."

He wouldn't take the ring. "This doesn't make any sense," he said. "When will you be ready? When Derek comes back from his mission? When Megan graduates from high school?"

"I don't know."

"Why is it that everyone else's needs come ahead of mine?"

"It's not only Derek and Megan. Right now marriage seems like a trap that will take over my life and cause me to fulfill everyone else's needs without having time to see to my own. That's what has happened to my mom all these years. I'm just not ready for a commitment like that. Besides, I wouldn't make you very happy if we got married now. Really, it's better this way. I'm not going to end up like my mother. Do you know how much she makes now? A college graduate can earn three or four times more. I have to be prepared to raise my kids if my marriage ends in divorce."

"Your marriage isn't going to end in divorce."

"You don't know that for sure. Who can say what the future

holds? It happens all the time, Ben. Just look around. In three years I'll graduate. Maybe then I'll be ready."

"Three years? Are you out of your mind? I can't wait three years."

"I'd wait for you that long if you asked me to."

"Well, I'm not you."

"What is it with you? If your woman doesn't satisfy your needs, then you dump her and find someone else. Is that how it goes with you? I mean, that's what my dad did, and that's what you're about to do with me. Well, walk out on me and find someone else then. You don't care about me or my feelings. All you care about is getting what you want. So how are you any different from my dad?"

"You have no right to say that."

"Why not? My mom suddenly isn't young enough for him so he dumps her. I tell you I can't marry you right away and so you're about to dump me. I can't see there's much difference between the two of you."

Out of his frustration and anger, Ben hit the wall with his fist and, much to his surprise, put his hand through the plasterboard. They both looked at the caved-in hole in the wall of the living room.

"I can't talk to you now," he said and then left.

"What'll it be?" Anne asked at six o'clock the next morning at Jiffy Buns Donut Shop.

"Donut and orange juice," Ben said, his elbows on the counter, his head in his hands, his eyes nearly closed.

"You're up early this morning."

"Never went to bed," he muttered.

"What kind of a donut do you want?"

"I don't care, any kind."

She set his order down in front of him.

"It's all over between Kimberly and me," he said.

128

"Kimberly said you had an argument, but does that mean it's all over?"

"It's over. That's what she wants." He paused. "I came here to apologize. I'm sorry for putting a hole in your wall. I can fix it today if you want, while Kimberly is on campus."

"There's no hurry."

"I don't know what came over me. I guess you know she broke off our engagement."

"Yes. She told me she needed more time."

"I guess I could have taken that, but then she accused me of being just like her father. That's not fair. I'm not like him. That's when I put my fist through your wall. Sorry."

"What's going to happen now between you and Kimberly?"

"I don't know. I think she wants me out of her life."

"I'm not so sure about that. She was pretty broken up after you left last night."

"Well, that's good news," Ben said with just a hint of a smile.

"And, if it's any consolation, if I could pick anyone to be Kimberly's husband, you'd be my first choice. But, even so, Ben, you've got a lot to learn."

"I do?"

"Yes."

"And Kimberly doesn't?"

"No, Kimberly has a lot to learn too."

"How can anyone eat a donut at this time of day?" he said, pushing the plate away. "What do I need to learn?"

"You need to learn to listen with your heart."

"You sound like one of those articles in a women's magazine my mother buys at the grocery store."

"You read women's magazines?" Anne teased.

"Not really."

"It might do you some good actually."

"I doubt it. What does listening with my heart mean?"

"It means that if Kimberly is upset about something, you

129

don't rush in to solve the problem until she's told you how she feels."

"Give me an example."

"This morning when I came to work, I tried to turn on the dishwasher and nothing happened."

"Did you check the circuit breaker?"

"Sorry, Ben, you just flunked."

"What are you talking about?"

"You jumped in with a solution to my problem."

"What are you talking about? Checking the circuit breaker is the first thing you do when you've lost power."

"Go home and get some sleep, Ben. If you ask me, you should have read more of your mother's home magazines."

"First Kimberly's on my case and now you."

"But don't ever forget I'm on your side, okay?"

He paid for his food, then returned to his apartment and went to bed. He slept until noon, went to his one o'clock class, then came back to his apartment and called Jeni at his dad's store in Rock Springs.

"Jeni, this is Ben. How's it going?"

"Why are you calling me?"

"You're different from other girls. You're more like a man. I really admire that in a woman."

"Have you been drinking? Look, I'm not loaning you any money, no matter what kind of a jam you're in, so you can just forget it."

"I need some advice. You remember Kimberly? Well, she just dumped me."

"Find someone else then. Look, I gotta go. There's a guy here who locked his keys in his pickup, and he's due in court in fifteen minutes."

"That's it? That's your big advice? Find someone else?"

"What other choices are there? If she dumps you, you move on."

"Don't you want to know how I feel?"

"Good grief, man, what's wrong with you? You're not turning mush-brained on us, are you?"

"You didn't even let me explain how I feel."

"Look, Ben, I told you how to fix your problem. What more do you want? But now I've got to go. You're not the only one around here with problems." She hung up.

Ben felt like it had been a mistake to even call Jeni. *She doesn't even care about me,* he thought. *She didn't even listen to me.*

It was then that what Kimberly's mother had said suddenly made sense to him.

Later that afternoon Ben showed up at Kimberly's home to fix the hole he'd put in the wall with his fist. Derek let him in. Ben was all primed to listen to Kimberly's feelings and let her know once and for all how truly sensitive he had recently become.

She didn't come home until he was nearly finished. She walked in the door, saw him, and said, "Hello."

"Hello."

"Doing a little repair work?" she said.

"Yes. How was your day?"

"It was okay."

"You felt good about your day then, is that right?" he asked, trying to apply what he'd learned from her mother.

She looked at him strangely. "I just said that, didn't I?"

"Yes, of course."

"Are we still singing Friday and Saturday night?" she asked.

"How would you feel about it if we did?" he asked.

"The money's good. If we possibly can, let's do it, even if things between us aren't the way they used to be."

"All right then, it's settled."

"I need to give you back some things," she said.

"What things?"

"Some tapes and . . . your ring."

131

Ben panicked. This telling how you feel was harder than it looked. All his life he had grown up with the image of the strong, silent man who takes on the world and never complains, and now, all of a sudden, it seemed like the rules had suddenly changed and he was supposed to be weepy and sentimental.

It was too much to ask in such a short time. "Well, if you're not going to use it, I might as well get it back. It cost me a lot of money."

"I'm sure it did. I'll go get everything and come right back."

While she was gone, he practiced in his mind what he would say to her when she returned. *I feel bad we're breaking up. That's good,* he thought, *because it's honest and it shows I'm a sensitive kind of guy. And I do feel bad we're breaking up, but of course it's mostly Kimberly's fault this is happening anyway.*

I feel like this is mostly your fault, was his second round of feelings, followed by: *I feel like you don't really care about me one way or the other,* followed by: *This is all your fault.*

That's right, he thought.

Kimberly came down the stairs and gave him the ring and tapes.

"I hope you're happy now," he said sarcastically.

He knew he'd blown it, but she made him so mad he couldn't think straight. So much for sensitivity, he thought. He left without another word, the ring in his hand.

The next morning he showed up at Jiffy Buns again.
"It doesn't work."
"What doesn't work?" Anne said.
"Listening with my heart. It doesn't do any good. She didn't want to tell me what was in her heart. All she wanted to do was give me back the ring."
"Did you tell her how you felt?"
"Yeah, sort of."
"What did you say?"

"I said, 'I hope you'll be happy now.' " He said it in a sincere voice, much differently than it had sounded when he had said it to Kimberly.

"Are you sure that's what you said?"

"More or less. Oh, what's the use? What I said was, 'I hope you're happy now.' " He said it the way he'd said it to Kimberly.

"My gosh, Ben, where'd you get your sensitivity training — from the National Rifle Association?"

"This isn't easy for me."

"How do you feel about the fact that you and Kimberly have broken off your engagement?"

"I feel like none of this would have happened if she — "

"Stop it, those aren't feelings. Feelings are more basic. People feel sad or angry or giddy or silly. Are you even in touch with your feelings?"

Two construction workers came in for a cup of coffee and a donut. Their presence threw a blanket over Ben's being able to talk about his feelings, because these were the kind of men he'd always looked up to — men who got things done instead of standing around wringing their hands and telling people how they felt.

The men left a few minutes later, but for Ben their influence lingered on.

"This morning when I came to work, I noticed the car was running hot," Anne said. "It kept getting hotter and hotter. I was afraid I wasn't even going to make it here."

"Could be a stuck thermostat," Ben said.

"You failed again, Ben."

"What?"

"You're supposed to say, 'That must have been frustrating.' Learn to listen with your heart."

"How long am I supposed to do that when I'm talking to someone?"

"As long as it takes."

"How am I going to judge that?"

She sighed. "All right. Listen with your heart for three minutes, and then you can go ahead and solve their problem for them."

He'd had enough for one day. He paid Anne for his breakfast and started to leave.

"Ben, listen with your heart, but also you need to tell Kimberly what's *in* your heart."

"Yeah, right."

"I know this is hard for you to learn, but it'll be worth it if you can learn it now." She paused. "Is there anything I should be working on, you know, as a mother?"

"You never have fun with your kids."

She gazed at him. He could tell she was thinking, and then she nodded her head. "Thanks. I'll work on that."

That night he wanted to practice on someone, so he called Jeni at home. "Hi, it's me again."

"I could tell."

"I've always liked you, Jeni. Oh sure, we've done pranks on each other, like the time I put a laxative in your hot chocolate, but despite it all, I always knew we were friends. I feel like underneath that hard exterior lies a wonderful human being. And I for one feel good about our friendship."

"You put a laxative in my hot chocolate?"

He hung up.

That night out of frustration he went out to a store and bought a copy of *Woman's Day* magazine. It didn't do him any good, although he did appreciate the helpful suggestions on cooking broccoli.

14

On Friday night, Ben and Kimberly went to Angelo's in separate cars. "I think it would be best if we didn't look at each other during the love songs," Ben said.

"What do you want me to do, look straight ahead?"

"Yes."

"Look, we have to act out a part here or we're both going to end up without a job, and I can't afford that because I really need the money."

"Just don't look at me on the love songs, okay? Nobody will notice."

Angelo noticed. After the first show, he came up to them. "What's going on? It was like a funeral in here. And whose bright idea was it to do 'Feelings' anyway?"

"Mine," Ben said quietly.

Angelo pointed at Ben. "You do that again, Mister, and you're both fired! Feelings, my foot."

"You didn't bring us a pizza," Ben said.

"Hey, you want a pizza, buy it yourself."

They ordered a small pizza and sat in wounded silence in a corner booth. They had forty-five minutes until their next show.

"Is that all you're going to do—play with the salt shaker?" Kimberly asked.

"I feel like crud," Ben said, in what he considered a supreme triumph of shared feelings.

"They say something's going around."

"It's not that."

"What is it then?"

He cleared his throat. He felt a rush of emotion, which he fought against, because he was afraid if he told her how he felt, it wouldn't make any difference, and on top of everything, she would think of him as a wimp. But, on the other hand, if he didn't tell her how he felt, then he might lose her, and he couldn't stand for that to happen. He had to do something to let her know how he felt.

"It's probably just a cold," he said.

"Drink plenty of fluids," she said.

"Yeah, sure."

He gave up on the salt shaker and stared at the pepper shaker.

"Oh, for our second show," Kimberly said, "a guy from my math class said he might come by to hear us. His name is Michael. I'll introduce you when he comes."

"Didn't take you long, did it?"

"He's just a friend. He and I are in a collaborative study group."

"Yeah, right."

"Look, from now on, what I do is my business. I don't have to answer to you. And one other thing, since you don't want me looking at you during the slow songs, I might take a microphone out in the audience and sing to Michael . . . just as a gag."

"Hey, sit on his lap, for all I care."

"Excuse me, I've got to get away from you for a while. You're such a grouch tonight."

The second show was a disaster for Ben. On every love song, Kimberly went out into the audience and picked out one of the guys to sing to. The first one she picked was her friend Michael from school. Ben quit singing and just stood there with his mouth open while she sang to Michael one of the songs they had written.

After two songs, Kimberly returned to Ben.

"Now we'd like to sing 'Feelings,'" Ben announced.

Angelo banged two empty pizza pans together to remind Ben what would happen if they sang that.

"No, Ben, we're going to sing, 'You are My Sunshine,' and we'd like everyone to join in," Kimberly said.

"You Are My Sunshine" saved them from being fired, but after the second show, Angelo went up to them and said, "When's the last time you two practiced together?"

"It's been a while."

"Look, either you come back tomorrow night with new material and a little life in your act, or you can go find yourself another restaurant to sabotage."

The next morning they met at nine at Kimberly's house and started practicing. They practiced until noon, and then Kimberly said she had been invited to lunch by Michael. She scheduled another practice for two o'clock and left. Megan and Derek invited Ben to have lunch with them.

"Kimberly still loves you," Megan said as she opened two cans of soup.

"How do you know that?"

"She told me."

"She's got a strange way of showing it."

"You're not much better. Why don't you tell her you love her?"

"Why should he do that?" Derek said. "I say if a woman crosses you once, then you dump her."

"Derek, you don't know a thing," Megan said. "And tuck in your shirt, will you?"

Ben and Megan sat silently for a while. Then Megan spoke up. "My bike has a flat tire."

A perfect opportunity, Ben thought, *to practice listening with my heart.* He set his watch to time himself for three minutes.

"That must make you feel really bad," he said.

"It's been like this for months."

"It must be so frustrating not to be able to use your bike when you want to."

"How about fixing it now while you're waiting for Kimberly to get back?"

"A flat tire can be very discouraging, especially when you're all ready to ride your bike and you go out to the garage and it's flat."

"Are you going to fix it or not?" Megan snapped.

Ben looked at his watch. Only forty-five seconds had passed. He couldn't see how anyone could go three minutes with this "listen with your heart" garbage. He gave up. "Sure, I'll fix it for you."

They ended up having to go the hardware store to get another tube. Megan went along with him for company.

"I hope things work out for you and Kimberly," she said in the car.

"Thanks. If they don't, can we still be friends?"

"Sure we can. I like you, Ben. It gives me an idea of what kind of a guy to look for when I get older." She paused. "I am going to get older too. I'm pretty sure about that now."

He looked at her strangely.

"For a while there, I was thinking about killing myself."

"You were? Why?"

"Because everything kept getting worse."

"I'd hate to think of a world without you in it."

"Yeah, I'm pretty sure I'd have ended up regretting it if I'd done it. The trouble with killing yourself is that you keep on existing even after you die."

"If you ever feel that you don't want to live anymore, promise me you'll call me, even if it's in the middle of the night. I'll come over and we'll talk. Okay?"

"Okay."

Ben and Derek and Megan were in the garage working on the bike when Kimberly and Michael returned from lunch. Michael pulled into the driveway. Kimberly stayed in the car and talked to him. They didn't know that twenty feet away Megan was looking out the small window in the garage and describing to Ben what was going on.

"She's smiling at him, like he said something really funny."

"Mister Collaborative Learning Group," Ben grumbled.

"You want me to help you waste this guy?" Derek asked.

"That wouldn't solve anything."

"They're getting out of the car," Megan said. "Now he has his arm around her waist while they're walking to the front door."

Ben was still working on the bicycle. Megan turned to face him. "You've got to do something, Ben, right away, or you're going to lose her," she said.

"Tonight for sure," Derek said.

"What?" Ben asked.

"Kidnap her and tell her you won't let her go until she agrees to marry you," Derek said.

"Is that the best you can do?" Megan said.

"You got something better?" Derek snapped.

"Ben, just let her know how much you love her," Megan said.

"What difference is that going to make?" Derek asked.

"Oh well, sure, Derek, your way is much better."

"I know that."

That night Ben gave Kimberly a ride to Angelo's. "After we finish tonight, could we spend some time together?" he asked.

"Sorry, Michael and I are going to study."

"Study, yeah, right."

"It'll be more than just Michael and me. There's two more in the group."

"How come this is the first time I've heard about this group?"

"We used to meet right after class, but one of the guys in the group can't meet then anymore."

"Are you the only girl in the group?"

"Yes."

"It figures."

"It just turned out that way."

Saturday night was always a big night at Angelo's. As they set up to play, Angelo came over. "You understand how important tonight is for you two, don't you? You mess up again like last night and you're finished." He stopped. "But, relax, have a nice time, make the customers happy."

"Are we going to look at each other tonight?" Kimberly asked Ben as they tuned up.

"I guess we'd better."

"I'd say so."

Their first show was a big success. Angelo brought them a pizza and put his hand on Ben's shoulder and said, "That's more like it. Keep it up."

They sat at a small table next to where they performed and ate. While she was eating, he said to her, "I'm always surprised at how beautiful you are. It's like I forget, and then I see you and it's the first time all over again."

Looking at each other again, for just a minute all the barriers were down and it was like the first day they met. But it wasn't their first meeting, and much had happened since then. He could see a sadness in her eyes.

She glanced toward the door and her expression changed, and he knew Michael had just walked in.

"Excuse me, I need to make a phone call," he said, getting up and starting to leave.

"Is it okay if Michael sits with us?" she called after him.

"Yes, of course."

He went to a pay phone in the hall and called Anne. "What's the one thing I can say to Kimberly that will make the biggest difference to her?"

"Can I talk to you before you leave with Michael?" Ben asked Kimberly after they finished performing for the night.

She put her guitar in its case and turned around. "Yeah, sure."

"Can we talk in my car?"

"Fine with me."

They sat in the car for what seemed like a long time before he said anything. Finally he began, somewhat hesitantly. "I know that you've had to go through some hard times lately . . . and . . . I understand that you're not sure if you're ready to get married now."

She sighed. "That's right, I'm not."

He spoke softly but with a little more confidence. "I just want you to know that I love you. There's never going to be anyone else for me except you. I know you need some time, so I've decided to work for my dad this summer at the store. I'll come down to see you whenever I can get away. And I'll be back for school in the fall." He stopped a moment, then went on. "I guess the main thing I wanted to say is, take as much time as you need. It's like this song I heard once. It goes, 'If it takes forever I will wait for you.' Well, that's the way I feel. I guess I'd better let you go study. Michael looks like he's about to fall asleep."

"Ben, thanks for being so understanding," she said.

"Sure, no problem."

She kissed him on the cheek and then left to go study with Michael.

15

That summer Ben's usual pattern was to take off after work on Saturday and drive to Utah. He'd get in late, stay at his aunt's house, go to church with her, and then show up at Kimberly's house for lunch. Then he'd leave Monday morning for Wyoming, arriving in Rock Springs just in time to go to work at one in the afternoon.

"What are you doing after work tonight?" Jeni asked the second Saturday in July.

"Driving to Utah."

"Again? My gosh, Ben, why don't you just buy yourself a bus and take passengers? You're on the road more than Greyhound."

"I suppose."

"Your sweetie still got cold feet about getting hitched?"

"Yeah."

"Can't say I blame her. You'll be lucky if you can find anybody who'll have you."

"Thanks for the vote of confidence, Jeni."

She paused. "Look, I know your weekends are filled up, but . . . look, just forget it, okay?"

"What's on your mind?"

"Well, I'm on a bowling team and one of the guys left town. You interested? It's Wednesday nights. Look, if you're not, it's no big deal. It doesn't matter to me one way or the other."

"I'm not much good as a bowler."

"That's okay. We're just in this for laughs anyway."

He smiled. "Sure, why not. Count me in."

The next week he went bowling with Jeni. She teased him unmercifully, but that was what he expected anyway. They ended up having a good time.

When he got home, his mother told him Kimberly had called while he'd been gone. He phoned her right away. He had planned on leaving Friday night because he'd worked at the store on the Fourth of July just so he could get an extra day off later in the summer.

Kimberly told him she'd be working until five on Saturday. She was working in the Mechanical Engineering Department. "Sorry, once we start the experiment we can't stop. You still want to make the trip?"

"Sure, no problem."

"Where were you when I called?" she asked.

"Bowling with Jeni."

"You know she adores you, don't you?"

"Jeni? No way. We're just friends—just like you and Michael are friends. Are you still seeing him every day?"

"We work together, just like you and Jeni do."

Ben drove to his aunt's house Friday night and slept in until noon on Saturday. Then he got up and worked around his aunt's place. At five o'clock he went over to Kimberly's. She wasn't home yet, so he sat around and talked to Megan and Derek and Anne.

"Derek has some good news," Anne said.

"What is it, Derek?"

"They're going to let me have my Eagle," Derek said.

"That's great. What made them change their mind?"

"Brother Hatch went around talking to people. He set up

a meeting for us to go to. I told them I was sorry for what I'd done."

"Are you glad you're going to get it?"

"Yeah, I guess so."

Derek stayed a few more minutes, then left to go out with some friends. Anne excused herself to go work in the kitchen.

"I keep telling Kimberly she's crazy for treating you so mean sometimes, but she never listens to me," Megan said. She talked with him for another fifteen minutes and then told him she was going over to a friend's house.

Anne called Kimberly's work number but there was no answer. She waited until eight-thirty and then told him she had to go shopping for groceries, but he was welcome to stay in the house and wait. At nine o'clock Kimberly arrived in Michael's car. She was wearing cut-off jeans and a T-shirt.

"I didn't think you'd still be here," she said as she walked into the house.

"What happened?"

"We finished the experiment early. Michael asked me to go up and see his uncle's cabin."

"Why would he want you to see his uncle's cabin?"

"Because the professor we work for asked Michael and me to be in charge of a party for our research group, and we had to see if it'll be big enough for us to use."

"And then what happened?"

"It was so pretty up there that we decided to take a hike. I guess we lost track of the time."

"Kimberly, thanks a lot. I've been waiting four hours for you to show up."

She didn't seem very concerned. "Sorry."

"Why didn't you at least call to say you'd be late?"

"Why do you keep coming around here anyway? I know it's just a matter of time. You'll end up leaving me sometime, so what difference does it make if it's now or later?"

"I won't ever leave you."

"You will. Everybody breaks up eventually. Since my folks' divorce, I've started noticing how many marriages are ending in divorce. It happens all the time."

"It won't happen to us."

"You want to know the truth about today? I wanted to hurt you," she said. "I wanted to make you so mad you'd quit coming around. It wasn't Michael's fault. He kept saying, 'Shouldn't we go back?' And I'd say, 'No, we have plenty of time.' I'm sorry. I don't know what got into me. All this week I've felt that if I made you mad enough, you'd break up with me and take up with Jeni big time. I just kept thinking it's better for us to break up now instead of after we're married and have two or three kids."

"I'll never leave you."

"You can't say that for sure. If we got married, we'd have problems. Everyone I know has problems in their marriage."

"We'll work out our problems."

"What if we can't?"

"Then we'll go to somebody for counseling."

"I'm not always going to look the way I look today. Someday I'll be old and fat and I'll have wrinkles."

"We'll get old together."

"But you'll always be surrounded by younger women where you work, maybe even your secretary, like with my dad, or someone else you work with." She sighed. "Oh, I'm so messed up. Look, I know what I'm doing to you isn't fair. I think maybe it'd be better if you didn't come to visit me for a while. I need some time by myself to work things out."

He looked at her for a long time and then said, "Whatever you say."

On Wednesday of the next week Kimberly called Ben just to talk. She told him that Brother Hatch had found a better job for her mother in the registrar's office at the university. It paid better, but the main advantage was that her hours allowed her to be home when her children were home. She'd also have more time to be available when prospective buyers came to see the house.

"Anything else happening?" he asked.

There was a long pause and then Kimberly said, "My dad and Gloria are getting married Friday."

"Are you going to the wedding?"

"No." She paused. "I'm really having a hard time with this."

"Why?"

"When my dad called to tell me and Derek and Megan about the wedding, he also told us Gloria is taking the missionary lessons. What if she joins the Church?"

"Would that be so bad?" Ben asked.

"I just don't think it's fair. My dad abandoned us because of Gloria. I don't think she should ever be allowed to join the Church. I keep thinking that in five years, they'll be living in some ward where nobody knows how they got together. When someone finds out he's been married before, they'll ask him about his first marriage and he'll say, 'It just didn't work out.' And nobody will know that it was my dad's fault. He'll make it sound like it was just something that happened, like when the leaves fall off the trees and there's nothing you can do to stop it."

"Maybe it wasn't all your dad's fault."

"I don't know. I don't know much of anything right now. My dad is moving on with his life. It's just the rest of us that are still stuck in the past. I keep thinking things are going to get better for me, but it's not happening yet. Somehow I've got to work this out."

"Your engine sounds like crud," Jeni said as she watched him drive into the parking lot for work one day. "You want me to help you overhaul it?"

"It's okay."

"We could work on it after work."

146

"Jeni, I still love Kimberly."

"And a whole lot of good it does you too, right? Now she won't even let you come down to see her."

"She's trying to work through some things."

"And what about you? The only time you smile anymore is when I'm on your case about something. So, what do you think about us fixing up your car?"

"Okay, thanks."

"Why should I get married when I know that every marriage has problems?" Kimberly asked Brother Hatch the next time he came home teaching.

Brother Hatch thought about it for a minute and then bent down and whispered something to Mike Jefferson, his companion. Mike got up and left without another word. "Mike will be back in a minute with the answer to your question."

"If I could know for sure that my marriage would end up as strong as yours, then I'd go ahead," Kimberly said.

"My wife and I have had our shares of disagreements and hurt feelings, but we never have thought of giving up."

Mike returned a minute later with a rose he'd cut from Brother Hatch's garden. He handed Kimberly the rose. It was a dark red and smelled wonderful.

"That's the answer to your question, Kimberly. You can't have a rose without some thorns."

She kept the rose in her room for days, and every time she saw it, she thought of what he'd said.

But somehow she wanted more assurance than that.

Kimberly woke up at six o'clock on that first Sunday morning in August. She was fasting and wanted plenty of time to be alone before she had to get ready for church.

She turned to the topical guide in her Bible and began looking up scriptures dealing with fasting. She worked her way down the list until she came to one reference that seemed to be exactly what she was looking for. She turned to Alma, chapter 17, which tells about the sons of Mosiah on their way to teach the Lamanites. "And it came to pass that they journeyed many days in the wilderness, and they fasted much and prayed much that the Lord would grant unto them a portion of his Spirit to go with them, and abide with them. . . . And it came to pass that the Lord did visit them with his Spirit, and said unto them: Be comforted. And they were comforted."

Kimberly kept reading until she got to chapter 26, where Ammon summarized their missionary labors among the Lamanites. " . . . we have been cast out, and mocked, and spit upon, and smote upon our cheeks; and we have been stoned, and taken and . . . cast into prison; and through the power and wisdom of God we have been delivered again."

The sons of Mosiah had been comforted by the Spirit to go ahead. And because they had gone ahead, even though they had difficult experiences, their lives had been spared and many people had been blessed.

Kimberly wasn't naive enough to think that there was a "one and only one" for her. There were probably many men whom she would be compatible with if she were married to one of them. And no matter whom she married, she knew problems would come up that both of them would need to work out. She knew there were no guarantees in life.

She had already talked to her bishop about how reluctant she was to get married because of what had happened to her parents. She had read several books about the family, she had talked with Brother and Sister Hatch about their marriage, and she had asked her mother for her opinion about what she should do. But none of what she had learned or heard was enough. She still felt uncertain.

There had been times in her life when she had felt the Spirit give her a feeling of calm when she was worried about something—when she was eight and had to play at a piano recital at her teacher's house; the day before school began when she had to go to a new school; when she had to sing the song she had written for her high school commencement — times when she had prayed and felt a comforting peace of mind.

She was dressed for church, but they didn't need to leave for another half an hour. She closed the door to her room, went to her bed, and knelt down. "Heavenly Father," she began softly.

It was not until sacrament meeting, while she listened to the testimonies of others as they related some of the blessings they had received in facing their problems, that suddenly, like a gentle breeze, she felt a calm spiritual assurance; and then, like the sons of Mosiah before her, she also was comforted.

Kimberly left Monday morning and drove to Rock Springs. She arrived in the early afternoon.

She walked into the hardware store and looked around for Ben. Jeni spotted her and came over. "What are you doing here?"

"I came to see Ben."

Jeni looked at Kimberly for a long time and then shrugged her shoulders. "Sure, it figures."

"What?"

"I just finished overhauling his engine."

"I'm sorry."

"Hey, don't apologize. The truth is, he's a pain. He's been taking up way too much of my time anyway." She stared at Kimberly again. "You've changed your mind, haven't you?"

"Yes."

"I could tell. Well, he's in the back. I'll show you."

In the supply room in the back, Ben was talking to two men about plastic pipe. Another employee was assembling a bicycle. "You got someone here who wants to see you," Jeni said, and then she walked away.

Ben and Kimberly stared at each other. "What are you doing here?" he asked.

She didn't want to open her heart up in front of all these people. "I wonder if you could help me. I'm looking for a monkey wrench."

He excused himself and led her into the main part of the store. "Don't they have hardware stores in Utah?"

"I like personal attention for my hardware needs. I was hoping I could get that here."

"We pride ourselves on personal attention."

"How personal?" she said without thinking, and then started to blush. "Sorry."

He looked at her strangely but didn't say anything. A minute later, in the plumbing supplies section, he said. "These are our monkey wrenches."

She hefted one of the wrenches. "Do the monkeys complain much?"

Their eyes met.

"Ben, what I really want is to marry you."

His mouth dropped open. "Uh . . . well . . . okay, but I have to work until six."

She smiled. "It doesn't have to be today."

The week before Christmas, Kimberly and Ben were married in the Jordan River Temple.

On their wedding night in their honeymoon suite, she waited for him to come out of the bathroom. He'd been in there a long time. She was starting to worry about him. Finally she went to the door. "Ben, is everything okay?"

"Yeah, sure. The toilet won't shut off completely. I thought I'd adjust the float. I'm almost done."

"Ben, listen to me. If you don't come out right away, then when we get back to Wyoming, I'm going to tell all your customers that this is what you did on our honeymoon night."

150

He opened the door immediately. "Maybe I'll just finish it up later."

She sat in a chair with a guitar in her hands. "I'd like to dedicate this song to you," and she sang "A Wintry Night."

When she finished, he clapped. "Very nice. Encore."

"My encore is you, my life is yours, my love is true."

She set down the guitar and came over and kissed him.

"What you said rhymes," he whispered in her ear.

She was kissing his eyelids. "Not now," she said. "Later maybe, but not now."

"It could be the beginning of a new song."

"It is a new song, Ben. This is our song . . . and this is the first verse."